Is the difference between poverty and prosperity anything more than a matter of trust?

TRUST

DAINES L. REED

Printed in the United States of America

DLR Publications, LLC.

Paperback: 978-1-7340526-0-2

Ebook: 978-1-7340526-1-9

Trust

Edited by: Jessica Carelock

TRUST

DAINES L. REED

Dedicated to my daughters, Chelsey and Holly: You are already as powerful, courageous, and forward-thinking as the incredible women who have inspired this novel.

ACKNOWLEDGMENTS

The completion of this novel would have been wholly impossible without God's incredible grace and mercy. For that, I am utterly grateful.

Many thanks to the team at Warren Publishing: Mindy Kuhn, Amy Ashby, and Jessica Carelock for transforming my manuscript into the novel it was destined to be.

To my parents, Joseph and Carolyn Allen, and my brother, Joseph Jr.: Ours was a wild ride! Oh, the adventures we have shared. And, through it all, the three of you formed a hedge of protection around me that made it safe for me to dream, create, and exist in Peace. Without your love and support, I wouldn't have been brave enough to imagine writing my own book.

Mom, thanks to you, I cannot live without books! Thank you for nurturing my love for reading and writing. Thank you for all of those insightful book discussions. Thank you for lending me books and introducing me to all kinds of literature in all formats. You taught me to see beauty in words, and in doing so, you laid the foundation for this novel.

Abram Reed, my husband, you are an incredible motivator and problem-solver. Thank you for listening to me ramble on about my characters' lives. We spoke about each one as though they were real people, and you were instrumental in helping each of them (me) to work through their (my) issues.

Thank you, Creola Reed, for sharing your stories and introducing me to the Sou-Sou. But most of all, I thank you for showing me that everything we do and say can be done with love. You are a living testimony, and this novel was made so much better because of you.

To my dear friends, my first beta readers, Frankie Singleton, Erica Maye, Amy Urresta, Maryann Bryson, Mattie Alexander, and my mom, Carolyn: Thank you for reading through my earliest efforts. I can't imagine what you must have been thinking when I handed you that big stack of papers! Your suggestions, recommendations, and observations were invaluable. Your kindness, love, and objectivity kept me moving in the right direction without discouraging my creativity or injuring my ego.

To Aunt Pinky, Aunt Judie, Lela Alexander Littlejohn, Serina DelGuzzo, Cecilia Arzate, Vickey Bingham, Lavena Reed, Monica Reed, Ti-Ras Myers and the countless family and friends who always remembered to ask how my book was going: You can never know the value of your kind words and encouragement. You made me feel as though you were interested in my dreams. Every time that one of you asked that question, 'So, how is your book coming along?' you validated my dream. You believed. I cannot thank you enough.

To my friend, Dejuette Jackson: You were my first writing partner. The first friend who loved words as much as I did. You couldn't have known it back then, but you made me feel that writing was a cool passion to pursue. I think, without your friendship and comradery, I might not have ever shared my work with anyone other than my mom. Thanks for the ride or die years.

Lorina V. Noble: Thank you for introducing me to everyone who we met as My Friend, Daines, the Writer. Thank you for getting me scraps of paper and tissue whenever I needed to scribble something down, right now, no matter where we were. You believed in my talents and made me feel as though I might be Carrie Bradshaw one day! If we ever make it to New York again, the Cosmopolitans are on me.

To my readers, to YOU: This novel is more than just a book. It is the tangible result of what happens when God tells you to put your butt in the chair and write. I wrote! And I'm honored to share my work with you. Thank you for your purchase. I hope you will enjoy it.

"For I know the plans I have for you, declares the Lord, plans to prosper you and not to harm you, plans to give you hope and a future."

—Jeremiah 29:11
New International Version

"… him whose purse is empty does gold avoid."

—George S. Clason

CHAPTER ONE

There is an undefined space where time seems to simultaneously move quickly and slowly. A space where a lot can take place in a short period of time, even in the absence of any perceptible visual evidence. It is the moment when the mind peels itself out of the realm of sleep and begins to shift into the realm of consciousness. These are the moments just after we have awakened, but have not yet opened our eyes. First, the mind wakes up, and then it slowly instructs the eyes, limbs, and other senses to follow the lead.

For some people—perhaps for most people—this is a peaceful time. It is the precious moment that signals the day's first deep breath and sometimes forces the body to stretch out and release itself from the contorted positions of slumber or to roll over and snuggle deeper into the covers before the eyes open to greet the new day. It is the instant when the nose begins to recognize the smell of fresh coffee in the air, when the brain is trying to remember if today is a Monday or a Saturday, or when the feet are timidly searching under the covers to reconnect with last night's bedmate.

For Ruth, there was no peaceful dawning of a new day. She hadn't experienced that in a long time. For

Ruth, there was only the frenetic pounding of her heart inside her chest, a ruckus that began the instant her mind awakened. Without fail, she awoke feeling wild and frenzied, her heart banging around like a wasp caught in a glass jar, flailing itself against the top, bottom, and sides, contained against its will. Her limbs tingled with adrenaline and her mind raced to take control of her body as though there were a chance that someone else might get to it first. Each time she awoke, an incredible pressure pulsed through her body and raced up her neck as though it could burst out of her ears, and she found herself torn between urges to either faint or vomit.

Today, in the milliseconds before her eyes flew open, she had already performed a self-assessment: *Where am I? Am I okay?* In the space of that fast and slow moment, she became aware that she'd slept in an awkward position and would likely have to deal with a crick in her neck all day. Her fingers found the thick wooden handle of the hammer underneath her pillow and her elbow was smashed into the thin pages of her Bible. Years ago, Ruth had adopted the habit of sleeping with the Bible tucked beneath her pillow, though she often discovered that it had migrated into the tangle of her bedsheets by morning. She remembered she had locked and barricaded her bedroom door, and she recalled she had packed her gym bag before she laid down for sleep last night.

After the assessment, she lay there on her back and thanked God for granting her the mercy of another day. She couldn't help but laugh to herself for the irony of her own thoughts. She was thankful for the new day, yet she didn't want to open her eyes because she knew that she'd actually have to get up and face it.

Covers off, feet on the floor, and she was moving toward the bathroom. Her body seemed to move by the sheer force and momentum of habit. Shower, brush teeth, wash face, push the soft afro back with a headband. Pull on scrubs and clogs and lanyard. Refill pockets with yesterday's loose change, a crumpled receipt, a post-it note, an ink pen, cherry ChapStick. Jacket, purse. Unplug phone from charger, slide it into the cargo pocket on one side of scrub pants. Hand on bedroom doorknob and— deep breath. *He best not mess with me this morning. Not today, Lord.*

But she could hear his snoring coming from the front of the house and she could hear the enthusiastic voices from an infomercial blaring down the hallway. Something about a blender that could make perfect margaritas and also puree organic baby food. If he couldn't hear the chime of the commercial's countdown clock, warning that you'd better call now to order the World's Greatest Blender before they're all gone, then he surely wouldn't hear her leaving for work.

Despite the apparent depth of his slumber, she moved down the hall and toward the front door with a skillfully silent swiftness, grabbing her keys from the hook, but briefly pausing at the door. After a moment, she doubled back into the kitchen to refill his pill box with a week's worth of colorful pills. The small plastic box, with seven compartments, each denoting a different day of the week, had been her attempt at helping him to remember to take his medications each day. She doled out his water pill, cholesterol pill, fish oil, multivitamin, and baby aspirin according to the doctor's orders, but she'd stopped administering the blue pill—the one he called his "nature pill"—quite a while ago. Without any affection or intimacy in their marriage, she had made the executive decision to eliminate the blue pill from the lineup.

In the car, with the house shrinking in the rear-view mirror, she thought about last night. It hadn't really been much different than any other night. On her way home from work, she had seen him standing in front of that trailer down the road where the guys hung out to drink and smoke in the evenings. She knew from experience that he wouldn't be home for a while. And then he had called, drunk and cussing, fussing about something and giving her advance notice that he was gonna see her when he got home. She was accustomed to his coming home drunk and had learned to stay out of his way until he eventually passed out on the couch. She had come to take his violent threats more seriously lately. The humiliation and intimidation reached a new level of audacity, even after all these years.

Last night, wisely, she planned ahead. She'd holed up in her bedroom, armed herself with a hammer and her Bible, blocked the door with a dresser, and prayed herself into a restless sleep. Even if she managed to rest well, her morning anxiety attack had brought the tension right back to the surface. She looked forward to the escape that work provided, her afternoon workout, and the brief nap that she would take in the physician's on-call room before she began the overnight one-to-one shift. She slept more comfortably at work than she did at home anyway, and she counted that as a small blessing.

Before she had wrestled her locker open, Irene was already getting Ruth caught up on the latest gossip. "Honey, you missed a hot mess out there at the community center last night! Well, you know we had the fish fry out there to raise money for Mr. Solomon's funeral services—word on the street is that the family can't afford to bury him, but his niece told me that the money he had set aside for his burial is tied up because they're all fighting over it.

"Okay, so, everybody was out there, getting things set up, and here comes Cynthia pulling up in the car with Deacon Turner. So, you know those girls from the singles ministry started making eyes at each other as soon as the car pulled up. Everyone had been saying they were dating, even though he kept denying it. They sure looked like a couple in love to *me*. Well, honey, he drove up in his mama's raggedy old Crown Victoria—and shame on him—a grown man driving around in his mama's car! From what I heard, he couldn't afford the insurance on that Lexus he used to drive, which is why he had to let it go back. Now, his credit is so messed up that he can't get approved for another car.

"Anyway, when he parked, Cynthia stepped out of the passenger side looking like she was Michelle Obama or somebody, but Deacon Turner didn't get out of the car." Irene's eyes sparkled mischievously.

Irene was no amateur storyteller and she knew how to control the tone of her voice or the speed of her words to build suspense. When she had your full attention, she would pause dramatically and try to make you guess what happened next.

Ruth, uninterested in the gossip and only partly listening as she pulled on her lab coat and shoe covers, entertained Irene with the appropriate response, "So what was the problem?"

"Honey." Irene had a knack for drawing out each syllable in the word in a way that seemed to form an entirely new phrase: *Huh-nee*. "He couldn't get the old car to shut off! He sat in there for about thirty minutes, trying to turn it off. When he finally got out of the car—*with the key in his hand*—that old car just kept on smoking and sputtering and stuttering. All the men were crowded around, looking under the hood, trying to figure out why a car would keep running without the key in the ignition. Personally, I think that car is just so old and has so many miles on it that it couldn't shut off, even if it wanted to! I actually felt bad for Cynthia. She had looked so proud when they first drove up. They ended up having to catch a ride home with the pastor.

Talk about embarrassing!

"So, honey, you know when she comes in today, she ain't gonna be nothin' to fool with! I hope you got your timecard in and your equipment checklists ready because, honey, she's gonna be a piece of work today!" Standing at the supply closet pulling out two clinical bouffant caps and passing one to Ruth, Irene continued babbling away, "And I meant to tell you, we raised a good bit of money out there at the fish fry, but not enough to bury poor Mr. Solomon, so somebody was talking about setting up an account on the internet to take donations for the rest of his burial expenses. The whole thing seems a little suspicious to me, to be honest. Our ministry hosted the fish fry, and somebody from that shopping center where he used to play Santa Claus every year is handling the donations, but I ain't heard a word out of his actual family about why he didn't have a burial policy or what happened to all his money. They always want to be seen flossin' around town, but can't afford to bury their own daddy? What do you think that's all about?"

Ruth tucked her hair into the cap and shrugged a shoulder, "Ain't no telling."

Mumbling more to herself than to Ruth, Irene rubbed on a fresh coat of lipstick, lips still moving, "Well, I don't know what it is either, but honey let me tell you something—I better not see anybody from that family today! I'm out there yesterday, sweating over hot fish grease, and then I still had to work at that durn group home last night," she paused to blot her lips, "and I ain't had no coffee yet." She puckered her lips together and approved her own reflection before moving away from the mirror. "So, I wish somebody would try me today!"

A few moments later, Cynthia walked in. Ruth noted that she didn't look anything like a woman who had been stranded in the parking lot last night with a broken-down date, or someone who'd been forced to bum a ride home with the pastor. She looked flawless. A little subdued, but as pretty and as fresh as always. A perfectly sewn-in bob, a modest-looking Merona slacks and blouse outfit from Target, full makeup, and a trying smile. The kind of smile that looks like it's trying to convince *you* when it can't even convince its owner.

As she made her way into the small break room, the space immediately seemed crowded. Cynthia had always been somewhat full-figured—and on more than one occasion Irene had whispered that she ought to quit bending her elbows quite so much—but she carried her weight well. She reminded Ruth of the old days when the healthy-looking, big-legged body image represented the physique that every woman envied.

Although only in her late 30s, Cynthia was often the subject of small-town gossip, as the local women speculated about when she would settle down or why she couldn't seem to keep a man for long. She was rumored to have dated a sampling of men from the church, but she knew how to keep her business to herself which provided little fuel for Irene's active imagination. As Cynthia was putting her lunch bag into her locker, Irene squeezed past her toward the hallway, mumbling something about getting some coffee.

Ruth caught Cynthia's eye and smiled mildly. While she often entertained Irene's gossip, she had long since learned not to take it as the Gospel. Irene did have a knack for getting the inside info, but she also had a tendency to embellish the details with wild flourishes, ad libs, and unfounded speculations. Whatever had gone on at the fish fry last night had nothing to do with Ruth, so she'd made up her mind to treat Cynthia as though she hadn't already heard the morning gossip.

The tears that welled up in Cynthia's eyes and threatened to ruin her makeup in response to Ruth's simple acknowledgement suggested that there was at least a kernel of truth to the rumors Irene had reported. But Cynthia turned toward her locker to hide her face and the ladies honored an unspoken no-crying-at-work policy, so Ruth took the opportunity to avoid a situation that had the potential to be too intimate and emotional for this time of morning.

"Let me run down here and make sure Irene don't charge that coffee to my account ..." Ruth said to no one in particular, offering a flimsy excuse for escaping the awkwardness that had invaded the small room.

Ruth met Irene down the hallway, halfway to the hospital cafeteria. A cup of coffee in each hand, Irene handed one to Ruth and the two fell into step with one another.

"Well, you can thank old Gerald from maintenance for your coffee. Honey, he was down there in the cafeteria trying to flirt! He knows he's too old for me—not to mention he's married—but I appreciate the free coffee. And I told him he had to buy yours too." Irene raised her cup toward Ruth's as though they were clinking champagne glasses instead of cheap Styrofoam cups.

She continued rambling, "And I hope he don't want nothing in return. Last thing I need is another relationship. Honey, two husbands have been enough for this lifetime and the next! I can't take care of another one!" Irene walked a little closer toward Ruth and attempted to whisper from the side of her mouth. "Speaking of husbands, you didn't have to strangle yours last night, did you? I heard he was down there at the spot after work, so I know he was fired up by the time he got home. And honey, the way my bank account is set up, I wouldn't be able to bail you out of jail until the fifteenth if anything had popped off between you two!"

Irene laughed at her own sad-but-true joke, and then her voice became more serious. "No, I know you wouldn't put a hand on him, even though he probably deserves it. I bet you're still putting out his medicine, aren't you?"

Ruth smiled sarcastically in defense. "If something happened to him, I'd be in the same boat as Mr. Solomon's family—hoping somebody would donate enough money to help me bury him. I can't afford to pay for his funeral, so I guess it's just cheaper to keep him."

The two friends laughed together and kept walking because it was easier than having the real conversation in which Ruth would have to admit the truth: she didn't know why she was still laying his medicine out because he didn't even take it most days. She didn't know why she was holding on to a marriage that had long since been dead. And she didn't know how things disintegrated to the point where she needed a hammer and a Bible just to get a decent night's sleep.

She thought about leaving sometimes. Correction: she thought about leaving *ALL* the time. Thought about running away—especially now that her daughter was grown— fantasized about just not coming home anymore. Thought about killing him, how to get away with it. Thought about killing *HERSELF*, just to get away from him.

One day, in the early years when her daughter was just a toddler, she had bolstered enough courage to leave. She came to this bold resolution after he accused her of staring at some guy they drove past in the car. In an instant rage, he grabbed a handful of her hair and banged her head into the driver's side window—all while she was driving with her daughter sleeping in her car seat.

Back then, she was a God-fearing young woman who'd vowed to remain married to her husband forever, but her instincts begged her to leave before her baby girl became the target of his brazen violence. She'd begun saving some money and had placed a deposit on a small apartment near the hospital. She planned to get the new place situated for herself and her little girl with the extra money she would be earning at work after her ninety-day, new-hire probationary period was up. However, in the week before her ninety days was complete, she learned some information that caused her to immediately abort her plan: in order to leave her husband and take her daughter, she would have to appear in family court where the judge could likely order shared custody between the two.

The thought of subjecting her little girl to unsupervised visits with a sadistic monster ... she could never—*would* never—allow that to happen. Instead she taught herself to anticipate and deflect the various forms of abuse, often times placing her own small body between a red-eyed monster and a frightened little girl. And now, years later, her daughter safely living as a responsible and healthy adult, Ruth remained, held in limbo by fear. Afraid to leave and afraid to stay.

Sadly, she had never lived alone, had never spent one night alone in her own home or even in a hotel room. It seemed funny now, the embarrassing irony that she was virtually alone with him anyway. What could he do to protect her if something went bump in the night? Most nights, he was barely able to stumble through the house, piss down the side of the toilet, and get himself back to the couch before he passed out again.

She was lonely with him in this worthless condition. No, he couldn't protect her from the bogeyman. If anything, HE was the one who she needed protection FROM. Yet, somehow, the familiarity of their lonely dysfunction was still more comforting than the thought of walking away to face another, unknown kind of loneliness.

"Are you clean or dirty today?" The question sounded far away and startlingly loud at the same time. Ruth blinked and regarded the computer screen as though she was surprised to find herself standing in front of it. She'd done the morning routine with Irene so many times that she didn't even remember walking into their little office and over to the computer. It wasn't actually an office. It was more like a doorless closet where the computer, printer, and a small dry-erase board were kept, just off the side of the sterilization area. It was where she and Irene stood each morning to review the schedule for the day and prepare their strategy for keeping the surgical instruments and supplies ready for the surgeons.

Jokingly, she patted at two imaginary breast pockets, both hips, and her empty back pockets before finding her glasses on top of her head, nestled down in her hair. Putting the glasses on her face, she squinted at the screen a few times and then took them off again, hooking them between the buttons on her paper lab coat. "I can't even read the words on this screen! How are we supposed to see anything on this old thing?" She looked sideways at Irene. "Let me try your glasses."

Sliding the dollar store cheaters out of Irene's hand, she held them up and peered through the lenses like they were jewelers loupes. The words on the screen came into view. "I guess I need to get my eyes checked again. You can be clean. I'll be dirty."

They worked around each other with the comfortable and familiar rhythm of old friends. After working together in the sterilization room for almost thirty years, they were closer than family. They had held one another up and saw each other through just about all life's peaks and valleys. 'In sickness and in health' was how they often joked about their bond. They had survived some tough times together, some of them so painful that they could no longer be mentioned.

They took care of each other, offering support and tough love as needed, never requiring thank you's, paybacks, or IOUs.

Each day, they divided their sterilization duties into "clean" and 'dirty.'" Today, Ruth welcomed the opportunity to tackle the dirty side. That meant she would be responsible for cleaning and sterilizing all the surgical instruments and equipment that had been used the previous day or overnight. Tasks like emptying and refilling the ultrasonic solutions, loading the autoclave, breaking down and reassembling surgical equipment, running spore tests, and wrapping instruments were the other duties assigned to the "dirty" sterilization technician, and they required little interaction with the doctors or the OR nurses. Today, she welcomed the opportunity to work at her own pace, relatively unbothered.

"Well, alright!" Irene clapped her hands together. "My coffee done kicked in. Let's get this ball rolling." They fell into their familiar rhythm, Ruth breaking down yesterday's case carts and loading the instruments into the machine that she'd mistaken for a dishwasher back when she was a new employee, and Irene reviewing each surgeon's preference card and beginning to pull the instruments and soft supplies needed to restock the empty carts for the next day's surgeries. Both women hummed to the Motown oldies streaming softly through the speakers of the small radio that sat on the shelf in the corner of the room.

When she had finished her shift, Ruth walked next door to the YMCA and changed clothes in the locker room. She filled her water bottle at the fountain and grabbed a towel before heading toward the treadmills. Running was something she looked forward to. The way that it cleared her mind and gave her something easy to focus on was a relief. Even when she was as tired as she was today, it was as though her energy for running remained high. She had learned to put her legs on cruise control. Once she set her pace, she could run for as many as five miles without much effort. As long as she had decent earbuds so she could listen to the Temptations radio station on her Pandora account, her legs did just what they were made to do.

After her run, a few minutes in the sauna, and a shower, she put her scrubs on again and walked back to the hospital. She often picked up third shift hours as a patient safety attendant in the emergency room or psychiatric ward, and there was no need to drive all the way home when she could easily nap in the hospital's on-call room for a few hours. With her daughter out of the house and a husband whom she preferred to avoid, there was rarely any real reason to be at home at all.

CHAPTER TWO

The labor and delivery unit had the best on-call room in the hospital, in Ruth's opinion. The room itself was sparse and non descript, just a couch and recliner, a small restroom with a shower, and a scuffed wooden desk in the corner. There was no television, no pictures, and no decor. What attracted Ruth to this room was the close proximity to the constant sounds of life just outside of the room's door.

Rarely did she witness any pain or suffering on this floor, no terminal illnesses, no car crash victims, no trauma patients. There was no bereavement suite. This floor had certainly seen its share of heart-breaking stillbirths and breath-halting delivery complications, but on most days, she could count on the atmosphere being full of life and expectancy. The irony of the thought didn't escape Ruth. The women on this floor were literally "expecting" babies, but, to a greater degree, she was drawn to the overall expectancy of good health, joy, and bright futures that charged the atmosphere in this part of the hospital.

She wrote her name and the length of time she planned to make use of the room on the clipboard that hung outside of the room's door, grabbed a fresh blanket from the warming station, and slipped quietly into the tiny oasis. Technically, this room was reserved for the on-call surgeons and the critical care nurses who needed to sleep, but she often slept here between shifts and had never been told that she couldn't. Since the hospital recently outfitted a state-of-the-art "sleep room" at the other end of the corridor, it seemed that most of the surgeons abandoned this unremarkable room in favor of the one with the most amenities.

Turning off the lights and closing the door, she curled up on the well-worn couch and pulled the warm blanket over her shoulders before tucking it under her chin. Just inhaling the clean warmth and freshness of the blanket evoked a calm and peaceful feeling. She was comforted by the noise and the constant activity coming from just beyond the room's closed door; phones ringing, nurses holding conversations in the hallway, babies crying, voices over a loudspeaker, the rumbling sound of one cart after another being rolled down the hallway. Anyone else would have found it too noisy for decent sleep. But for Ruth, the noise, the movement, the corridor lights filtering in around the edges of the closed door provided her with a peculiar sense of security. For her, it would have been silence and pitch blackness that would have made it too noisy to sleep.

A woman was crying—screaming, really—in the hallway. The sound was so broken, so pitiful. *Guttural*, maybe. That was a word Ruth had never used, although she read it in books and understood it in context. She had never taken the time to think about what it meant until now. From the gut, from the base of the stomach. If that's what 'guttural' meant, then it was the only word even loosely appropriate enough to describe the sound. The sound of a woman's heart breaking.

There's a difference, Ruth thought to herself, between the sound of the cry that is heard *after* a woman's heart has already been broken, and the sound of the cry that is heard as the breakage is actually occurring.

Like a person with two brains, Ruth was thinking about the words that best described the sound, and she was also realizing that no one had come to comfort the obviously devastated woman.

Blanket still around her shoulders, she crept to the door of the on-call room and peeked into the hallway. The young woman was down on the corridor floor, sitting against the wall, legs outstretched, hugging an empty baby carrier. The carrier looked as though the baby had just been in it with the safety harness dangling, blanket halfway in the cradle and halfway on the floor—as though someone had simply taken the baby out to go and change its diaper. But she was hollering, "He ruined my life! He ruined me! He stole my life!" She rocked side to side, clutching the empty baby carrier, completely unaware of her surroundings. *Her surroundings.* Ruth realized no nurses were around, no movement was in the air. There was no help.

Mid-holler, the young woman, not more than twenty years old, looked up, caught Ruth's eye and begged for help. "He's in there! Please ma'am, I'm not strong enough, but HE IS IN THERE. Please, ma'am, you know this ain't right!" Suddenly, the girl was up and dragging Ruth toward a closed door, midway down the hall. When she flung the door open, he WAS in there. Ruth's husband was in the room, surrounded by baby things, but there was no child in sight.

Their bursting through the door caught him by surprise, and he paused to look up from the cardboard box that he was digging through. Baby clothes, pictures, and other random items were strewn about, as though he had been ripping them from the box and flinging them aside in search something incredibly important. His expression of surprise turned into one of snide amusement as he saw the faces of the two women in the doorway. "The hell y'all want?"

"Do you have her baby?" Ruth was paralyzed in the doorway, hot, confused, sick-feeling—and at the same time, feeling ferociously protective of the young woman who had somehow let Ruth's husband get his grungy hands on a precious, innocent baby.

Ruth's thoughts were reeling, tumbling one over the other, faster than she could process them. *Who would let him touch their baby?* No sooner had that thought entered her head than it was joined by another: *why would he want someone's baby or any of their belongings in the first place?* She was shouting now, "You better give this girl her baby!"

A shameless, unbothered smirk unfolded across his face, spreading from his lips to his eyes. He looked as though he were about to shrug his shoulders, raise the palms of his hands in surrender, and say *'Okay … you got me … '*

Ruth was on him in that moment, hands around his throat, squeezing, digging, fully intent on killing him if it meant getting the girl's baby back. He didn't struggle, but she was keenly aware of how long it was taking for the smirk to fade from his face. Much longer than it took in the movies. But she kept on choking him, hollering at the girl like a drill sergeant: "Look around! Look for your stuff!" In the chaos, her thoughts became disconnected from her words. *Your stuff? Wait, no, your baby! Find your baby!*

She was screaming hysterically, and the girl was motionless in the doorway, still holding onto the stupid, empty carrier. He wouldn't die, and she wouldn't even try to find her own baby. Ruth's limbs were flooded with adrenaline; her heart was flailing around in her chest like a raging, caged beast. She was overcome by a wave of heated nausea. She realized that she couldn't feel her fingers.

And then she was awake.

The blanket was wrapped around her fingers like Chinese handcuffs, cutting off her circulation. Releasing her grip on the tangled blanket, she felt the blood flow return to her fingers again, chasing away the frigid numbness. Then, unsure as to how long she'd been sleeping, but knowing full well that falling asleep again would be an impossibility, she pried herself out of the crevice of the couch and sat up.

Reaching for her cellphone, she checked the time. She'd been asleep for twenty-three minutes.

CHAPTER THREE

Ruth got up from the couch. Once she had her shoes on and slid her cellphone in her pocket, she turned to straighten the cushions and fold the blanket. When she stepped out into the corridor, the energy on the floor was lively and untroubled, everyone completely oblivious of the horrific nightmare that she'd just experienced on the other side of the on-call room door.

Walking into the elevator, she smiled when she saw that Julene, one of her favorite CNAs, and Vincent, the third-shift maintenance technician, were already inside.

Ruth pressed the button for the emergency room floor and Julene said, "You're not going to the staff lounge? One of the drug reps sent a bunch of pizzas, salad, cookies, everythang! And they sent some of that good sweet tea from Burton's Restaurant. You better go get you some before the doctors get it! They always think everything is for them. Shoot, we do all the work!" She smiled at Vincent and winked, "You know it's the truth!"

The invitation reminded Ruth that lunch had been hours ago, and the handful of almonds that she'd eaten after her run was a poor substitute for real food.

"Yeah, I'll walk down there with you." She tossed a weary smile toward Julene and Vincent. "I brought some food from home, but I can save it for tomorrow. Let's go. I have some time before my shift starts."

By the time the trio arrived in the staff lounge, it was obvious that everyone else had already ravaged the free food. There were a few corners of cheese pizza left and a couple of oatmeal raisin cookies on a platter. No sweet tea. But the salad was barely touched, and Ruth was okay with that. She wasn't big on pizza, but the salad would be better than the frozen Lean Cuisine that she had brought from home, and she preferred to eat lightly anyway. As a one-to-one sitter, staying up all night long in the same room with the same patient could be grueling if your stomach was full and you were sleepy.

"Well, I'll be damned!" Julene was fussing. "They coulda left us something! What can a salad do for all of this?" She imitated a sexy pose and ran her hands down both her hips while she made pouty lips. "I got to eat some MEAT!"

Ruth laughed with her, winked at Vincent, and joked, "You might want to give that salad a chance if you want to keep that girlish figure. That's how I keep mine …" She stuck her own hip out and ran her hand down her side, giving herself a pat on the backside.

As she walked out of the lounge and back toward the elevator with her salad, she could hear Julene calling out to her from the lounge, "Uh-uh, Miss Ruth! Don't let me find out that the church lady used to have a freaky side!"

Before she reported to the emergency room, Ruth stopped at her locker to grab her sweater. The nurses back in the ER usually kept it uncomfortably cool on that side.

When she opened her locker, a slip of paper fluttered to the floor. She might have overlooked it, but the neon pink sticky note became stuck to the hem of her scrub pants on the way down.

As the administrative assistant for the hospital's human resources department, Cynthia was the one who ordered the office supplies, and she had a known obsession for anything brightly colored or covered in glitter. Apparently, she slipped the note through the vents of Ruth's locker, thinking that she was gone for the day. The note simply said: *Enrollment/ Elections?* In the bottom corner, Cynthia had written *Book Club?* in her bubbly, heavy-handed cursive writing.

Yes, they were supposed to pick a date and location for their next book club meeting, but the thing about the enrollment and elections must have been a mistake. Every year, the hospital employees were to fill out the form and state any changes that needed to be made regarding their insurance benefits or retirement contributions. Usually, this meant adding a new baby to your insurance or changing your last name after your wedding. Nothing had changed in Ruth's life in so long. She just signed hers on the day that it was given and slid it right back into Cynthia's mailbox. There was no need to take it home or spend much time thinking about it.

As she rounded the corner onto the back hall of the emergency room, Ruth assessed that the night was off to a quiet start. Her position was technically that of a safety attendant, but most of the hospital staff referred to it as the one-to-one, meaning that she provided one-to-one supervision for specifically designated patients. As a rule, if the patient entered the emergency room and stated that they were thinking of hurting themselves, they could not be left alone at any time, and Ruth ended up sitting in the corner of their room until another attendant could take over.

Some nights were more active than others, and the patients who were on this hall were typically dealing with mental illnesses, drug abuse, or attempted suicide. There were also the patients who were classified as high fall risks, escape risks, those who wandered intrusively, and those who were in restraints. Collectively, these were the poor souls who were weighed down by life's toughest challenges. These were people who needed professional help and couldn't be left alone to help themselves.

As the one-to-one sitter, Ruth did just that. She sat. She sat in the room with her assigned patient and watched them through the night. There was the occasional combative patient who didn't want to be confined to bed, and, in those cases, Ruth's only responsibility was to notify the nurse or call for security. However, on most nights, her patients simply wanted someone who would listen to them, pray with them, or stay up late to watch TV with them. Most were lonely, fearful, damaged souls who were more of a risk to themselves than to anyone else.

It wasn't uncommon that she was assigned to a patient who was so heavily sedated that they slept all night. Asleep when she got there and asleep when she left. She envied the depth and peacefulness of that kind of sleep—even if it had been artificially induced by clonazepam or lorazepam. If she couldn't enjoy that kind of rest, she was glad to see that someone else could. On those nights, she turned the room lights down to a low glow and read quietly.

She often found herself studying her sleeping patient, wondering what had happened in their lives to bring them here and wondering what types of dreams were unfolding in their minds. Tonight was one of those nights. Her patient was sleeping soundly, and the only interruption was from Julene who stopped in to refill the gloves, masks, and hand sanitizer.

Julene smiled when she walked into the room and saw Ruth. "What are you reading, Miss Ruth? Every time I look, you got a book in your hands. I would love to get my hands on a good book! I didn't get to read for fun too much back when I was a paralegal. I had to read so much for work that I couldn't stand the sight of a book after hours! But now that I'm at the hospital so much and running after the kids, reading a book sounds like a mini vacation from reality. Why haven't you invited me to one of your book club meetings, yet?"

That was Julene. She talked a lot, but she was friendly and down-to-earth, and she possessed a level of intelligence that often caught people off-guard. She didn't pay great attention to grammar when she spoke, and she liked to joke around most of the time, but she was educated and quickwitted. She had been a paralegal at one time and lived in Chicago to pursue her plans of becoming an attorney. But for whatever reason, she'd ended up back in town with a pair of six-year-old twin daughters, a five-year-old son, and a boyfriend who was content to be a stay-at-home father.

In a major career shift, she had taken the CNA certification class and picked up a job at the hospital rather than finding work at a local attorney's office. Now, instead of studying to be an attorney, she talked of going back to school to become a nurse and eventually, a hospital administrator.

The gossiping Irene was convinced that Julene had done something unseemly to get herself blacklisted from the legal community. Maybe there was something to that theory, but Ruth was more convinced that Julene was just one of those "failure to launch" people. Full of great potential, but mysteriously tethered to the ground, unable to take off in life for some unknown reason.

Ruth flipped her book over and showed Julene the cover. "It's my study bible. Our Sunday school class is in the Book of Ruth. Figured I should be the expert on that book." They cracked up quietly at the joke, realizing that it was now four in the morning and not wanting to disturb Ruth's patient. Regarding Julene a little more closely, Ruth spoke again, "I didn't know that you liked to read. You could have joined us a long time ago! I figured that you were too busy with the kids to get in on our extracurricular activities, anyway. When I talk to Cynthia in the morning and we pick the next club date, I'll let you know."

"Yeah, with three babies and a man at home, you'd think that I would be too busy. But he does everything for the kids. Honestly, I shouldn't complain. I know there are so many men out there who don't even try to help at home. But sometimes I feel like *I'm* the man in the relationship. Going out, working day and night, and coming home after he's already got the kids in bed or sent them off to school. He goes to all of their school events and field trips, does all of the housework—sometimes I'm looking at the Lord like, 'Are you sure that you didn't accidently give me a wife?!' I mean, the kids seem like they barely need me around. I almost feel like a stranger when I'm actually at home for any length of time. That's probably why I pick up so many extra shifts here at work.

"But I'm working like a Hebrew slave to support him and the kids, and he can't even afford to marry me. Like, he doesn't work, so if he bought me a ring, he would have to buy it with my money. Isn't that the same as me buying a ring for myself? That's not happening on a CNA paycheck. It's not like we really have a romantic relationship anyway. It's basically just an arrangement that kind of serves a purpose for both of us. I mean, if I put him out, who's gonna raise my babies while I'm at work? I wouldn't trust my babies with anyone except him. Maybe after I get my RN license, I can just work a couple of twelve-hour shifts and have the time and money to keep my own kids instead of being away from them every day and night." By now, Julene was giggling as she spoke. "But that's gonna take a while, so yes—please take me to your book club!" She was making an exaggerated pleading expression with her hands clasped under her chin. "It's not like I don't have a babysitter and I know y'all be in there sipping on some wine! Talking about a 'book club!' Uh-huh!" She made duck lips and shot Ruth a comedic, accusatory glance.

That, too, was Julene. Not one to dwell on her problems, she always found a way to lighten the mood with a joke. Though she was a little younger than the rest of the group, Ruth knew she'd fit in easily.

Chapter Four

Ruth didn't go home when her one-to-one shift ended. There was only an hour left before she'd be standing in the closet-office with Irene again. Thinking it better to just keep moving rather than let her brain find out that her body was tired, she walked across the parking lot to the Y again. She had planned for this and packed an extra set of scrubs, a toothbrush, her makeup bag, and some coconut oil for her hair. Sometimes she envied the way that professional women got glammed up for work, but on days like this, she welcomed the low-maintenance routine.

There was still time for coffee and some cereal in the gym's cafe before she needed to clock in for work. From the cafe windows that overlooked the lower level of the gym, her eyes scanned the early-morning warriors who were starting the day with a workout. She made a little game for herself by trying to guess which categories were most fitting for the people below.

There were a few people doing circuits in the corner, most likely a boot camp class. *The Diehards*. Some men were spotting each other at the free weights. *The Muscle Heads*. Three people were on the treadmills, all with earbuds stuffed into their ears, each one separated by a vacant treadmill. *The Loners*. There was a lady moving at an awkward pace on the elliptical and one guy reading the instructions for adjusting the settings on the rowing machine. *The First-Timers*.

This last group was easy to spot; they seemed uncomfortable and out of place in the gym. These were people who were trying to get into the "gym thing," had made New Year's resolutions, or were here to take advantage a two-week free trial membership. The woman on the elliptical was visibly struggling to get into a gliding rhythm and she was literally leaning onto the handlebars for support. The unnatural movements and her unbalanced stance made her rear-end jut out like a speed hump, each side lurching up and down in staccato, responding to the jerky movements of her legs.

Ruth remembered feeling like a foreign visitor during the early days of her gym membership, even though that had been almost twenty-five years ago. She sympathized with the woman and instinctively asked God not to let the woman give up. Not when she appeared to be trying so hard, even though she was clearly miles away from her comfort zone.

When the woman dismounted from the machine and turned around to leave, Ruth nearly choked on her coffee from the shock. It was Cynthia.

By the time Irene joined Ruth in the computer closet, Ruth was feeling pretty good. The combination of sleep deprivation and coffee always left her feeling a little silly and delirious. While most people might suffer from brain fog and irritability after working for almost twenty-four hours straight, Ruth usually felt high, the way that she imagined a happy drunk might feel just before they pass out. She'd struggle later in the day, but for now, she was in a great mood. "I can't hardly read the screen, so just pick clean or dirty, and I'll take whatever's left over," was how she greeted Irene. With raised eyebrows, Irene stopped tucking her hair into her bouffant cap. "Somebody pulled a one-to-one last night, I see. But, okay—I'll be dirty today. Cool?"

They smiled at each other. There was no wrong choice today. "Cool beans."

When they turned around to leave the computer closet, Cynthia was standing there smiling.

"So ..." That's how Cynthia began all of her work-related conversations. It's how you could tell if she was about to talk about an episode of the *Real Housewives* or explain the new changes to the employee manual. "It's open enrollment time and I have to get all of your paperwork in. I got yours," she said, looking at Ruth, "but you didn't check all of the boxes."

She pulled Ruth's sheet out of her bag and pointed to the section that referenced the employee stock holdings. "You have to pick one of these."

"I don't know what that part means. How ever they have it set up, that's how I leave it. That's why I never check the boxes. I never have." Ruth tried handing the form back to Cynthia.

"Okay, so I don't know why it wasn't caught before now, but they're auditing me, so I have to make sure that I submit everything correctly. Basically, this box," she turned the paper so that they could both see it, "this one means that you want to cash out any shares that you own, and this one means that you want to roll the shares over into something else. Now, don't quote me on that, but I'm pretty sure that's what it means."

This was a better explanation than Ruth had received in the past, but it didn't help much. She never understood all the stocks/bonds/shares jargon, didn't even know who to ask for help.

"Tell you what—I guess let's just roll it over. That sounds like the closest option to 'just leave it alone,'" Ruth said. She pulled a pen from the pocket of her scrub jacket and checked the corresponding box. "I don't even know what the stocks are. Who knows? Maybe I own this place by now," she glanced up at the stains in the ceiling where Maintenance was supposed to have replaced the tiles last summer. "It would be just my luck that I'd change the wrong thing and the IRS would show up, looking for me!" She smiled at Cynthia. "Okay. Enough of the business talk. Book club is next month. Are you hosting again?"

Cynthia discarded her professional smile and replaced it with a more relaxed one. "You know I'm hosting! I have some ideas for a themed meeting this time. It's a birthday month, so there's no book, but I thought of some ideas to make it a little different. Give us a taste of some culture. Wanna do the last Thursday of the month?"

They leaned over to look at the calendar that Ruth and Irene kept posted on the wall. The date was about five weeks out. "That would give me some time to get Mama situated," Cynthia murmured to herself.

Ruth looked over at her. "Don't you have home health going over there to take care of her?" That was none of her business and she immediately wished to take the question back. Working together, fellowshipping at church, and the occasional book club meetings provided just the right amount of social interaction between the two ladies, and Ruth had been careful not to become too familiar. She didn't like to intrude on anyone's private life and worked hard to prevent anyone from knowing too much about hers as well.

"I did," Cynthia sighed heavily. "The doctors say that she can live alone as long as she has help, but she won't let anyone help her except me. She runs every home health aide out of there within a week! And I don't blame them. I'm sick of getting cursed out by her, and I'm her own daughter. It's like she forgets that I'm her only child! Without me, she's alone. I can't imagine what she says to 'the help.' The Lord is going to have to bless me with an extra special man who could put up with a mother-in-law like that!"

Ruth changed the subject. "The end of the month works for me. Also, I invited Julene from the ER." Cynthia gave her a blank expression.

"Julene, the CNA? With the pictures of her kids hanging from her lanyard?" Ruth waited for Cynthia to make the connection.

Recognition spread across Cynthia's face then. "Okay, right. Her kids are so adorable. I can't believe she has THREE! She looks so young! She's so tiny."

An interesting observation about human nature occurred to Ruth in that moment: when people desire something or feel self-conscious about a thing they may be lacking, that's the thing they become most aware of in other people. Short people notice tall people. People with bad teeth notice people with great smiles. Single people notice married people, and married folks notice single folks.

Perhaps, to activate the Laws of Attraction, Cynthia noticed people in relationships who had children. That was her frame of reference as it pertained to Julene.

"Yes!" Cynthia said enthusiastically. "Bring her. The more, the merrier."

CHAPTER FIVE

When Ruth finally pulled her car into the driveway for the first time in almost thirty-six hours, the first thing she noticed was his feet sticking out of the back window of his car. He was asleep in the back seat, dressed in his work clothes, his boots strewn haphazardly on the ground beside the car where he'd apparently kicked them off before climbing inside. She could hear the radio streaming out of the passenger window.

Okay. Relax. She always steadied herself as she turned into the driveway that once led to her dream house. Once upon a time, this driveway had promised a different kind of future for her, but that all changed well before her marriage reached the "'til death do us part" stage. The driveway brought to mind a sermon her pastor had preached many years ago titled *The Road to Perdition*.

He explained that perdition was another word for hell or a state of destruction—a place where no good Christian would want to go. He warned the congregation that it was easy to find yourself traveling along the frightful road to perdition if you didn't stay aware. If you didn't remain vigilant.

His reasoning was that the road to hell was paved with good intentions that fail to come to fruition. *Things don't always turn out the way you intend*, he had preached. *You've got to seek God at all times, lest you find yourself floundering on a direct route to the pits of hell!* His preaching voice reached a shouting crescendo and then lowered until it was barely audible.

Then he leaned over the pulpit and whispered a critical warning: sometimes, the pits of hell can exist right here on Earth! He slapped his thick hand on the pulpit and slammed his Bible closed.

He stepped down from the altar and spoke for a while about the difference between good intentions and good works, about the pathway to perdition or the pathway to heaven, which eventually led to an open call to the altar for all who desired repentance. As the church organist began to play a soft tune to signal the end of the church service, Ruth's mind was fixed on the revelation that the road to perdition could appear in many forms. In her mind, her own driveway had come to represent the very pathway about which the pastor preached.

On most days, she could almost feel her car's hesitation as she pulled into the yard, as though it didn't want to go that way any more than Ruth did. She was sure that it wasn't her imagination. Home was no longer a pleasant place to be.

Her home had become a box of chocolates, and not Forrest Gump's box of chocolates, where you never knew what fun surprise you were going to get. The two of them alone in the house were those last two, unwanted pieces of chocolate that hadn't been gobbled up by anyone else. Without their daughter's youthfulness in the house to keep them distracted, their relationship had deteriorated to a condition that only divine intervention could repair.

They no longer slept in the same bed, rarely spoke, and led vastly separate lives under the same roof. Years ago, the state of their union had left Ruth feeling sad and depressed, but somewhere along the way, fear and loathing came to describe her feelings for him more appropriately.

Like a person with a split personality disorder, her husband alternated between being a violent, intimidating drunk, and a weak, sickly victim who couldn't care for himself. He was sick. That much she knew. But he was too mean, too unpredictable, and too unappreciative to even allow her to be the wife and friend she once was. To predict which person he would be on any given day was akin to taking a shot in the dark.

So, her habit was to prepare herself for whatever and whoever she encountered at the house each day. Today, it was him, sleeping in the car. Today, it was coming home to find out that the lights had been cut off. And, rather than do what a man should do—pay the bill, borrow some money, or even light a few candles—he did what was easiest for himself. He went to sleep in the backseat of his car.

Their financial problems weren't new. Things were always getting turned off. The bank account was always overdrawn. She couldn't tell anymore if his substance abuse and medical problems were the cause of their financial problems or the result of them. Ruth had long since given up on the idea of trying to save any money or plan for a future with him. He spent any money that accumulated in the bank and she was picking up one-to-ones just to keep up with the basic necessities.

To be fair, they were both terrible money managers. Always had been. Even though they had worked for their entire lives, living from paycheck to paycheck wasn't something that they'd grown accustomed to. It was the only way they'd ever known.

Alright. Cleansing breath. It's just me and you, Lord. Ruth held her breath as she moved from her car, past her sleeping husband, and through the front door. She set her intentions on two goals: food and sleep, relegating the lack of electricity to a lower position on her list of priorities. In the kitchen, she opened the refrigerator only to be greeted by darkness. Right. Thinking quickly, she felt around inside until she found the bowl of cut-up watermelon she'd prepared the other day, then grabbed a bottle of water before retreating to her bedroom. Safely inside, she closed and locked the door and lit a candle.

In her sleep deprived condition, all she wanted was rest. Lights or no lights, she was exhausted. Her direct deposit would hit at midnight, so she called the automated system and set up a payment arrangement to restore the electric service by morning.

Hammer under the pillow, she curled up on the bed. She could feel the Bible, still lying open, pressing into her lower back. She wouldn't be able to read it by candlelight, but it had become her bedmate and she was comforted by its presence.

Although she could hear the music coming from his car, the house was unbearably still and quiet. She felt around on the nightstand for her earbuds, pressed them into her ears, found Gladys Knight on Pandora, and pulled the blanket over her legs. Her stomach rumbled, and she pushed a barely-cold piece of watermelon into her mouth before turning over to find a reasonably comfortable position. In this moment, her need for sleep took priority over her stomach's request for real food.

She lay in the dark, staring at the ceiling and wondered how long she'd have to wait before sleep would come.

The little boy from next door was banging on the floor with the hammer. He banged and banged the hammer into the floor as though he was intent on digging a hole to China. He worked with surgical concentration, creating a gaping hole in her bedroom floor, seemingly unfazed by the odd group of people who were now gathering in the room around him.

Although the sound of his banging a giant hole in the floor was maddening, she was more outraged by the fact that he might have moved her hammer from under her pillow. *How had he even found the hammer in the first place?*

Looking around, everyone was in her room—the new surgeon from the hospital, Irene, people from the church, Julene's children—all of them now banging their own hammers. In a panic, she flipped her pillow over. The space where her hammer belonged was empty.

She searched frantically, hands moving across the sheets in the way of a person trying to read a page of Braille, checking every crevice in case she had overlooked it. The sound of everyone's banging was becoming stronger, starting to come together in sync. And then her heart was thumping around in her chest with the offbeat cadence of a sneaker in a clothes dryer and she was up and out of bed, running toward the door where her husband was banging on the other side.

Fumbling in the dark, Ruth realized she must have forgotten to push the dresser in front of the door. He was yelling, "Why you got this door locked? Who you got in there?"

He was coming in. She was nauseous. "Wait, baby—I was asleep, let me …" The door flew open and he was standing there, an immeasurable dark shadow. And then he had her pinned against the wall, jacked up by the front of her shirt, causing her feet to leave the floor, his knuckles digging into the delicate border of her jawbone, her chin.

"Why you ain't come home last night? I'm sitting in here in the damn DARK, and you ain't brang yo' ass home? Gone lay up with some dude? And I don't want to hear no shit about you was at no church all night!" He was growling, sounding like a crazy person, his words rhetorical and convicting. He smelled like pennies and stale beer.

"I was at work! I had to work! I told you that the other day. You know I had to do the sitter shift! What is wrong with you?" Ruth tried desperately to appeal to his senses of reason and logic, knowing that it was a worthless effort because he was the definition of raging insanity in this moment. Time was moving fast and slow, as it often did. *Why does he smell like pennies?*

The musky, metallic smell flooded her nostrils at the same moment that she felt the cold, rough metal blade dragging along her cheek, becoming tangled in her hair. Holding his wife suspended above the ground with one hand, he was trying to shove a rusty, broken machete into her face with the other hand, but he was having trouble adjusting his grip to the awkwardness of the long blade. Each time he brought it close to her face, the tip snagged her hair and thwarted his efforts. Each time the blade snagged, he'd jerk it away and draw it back toward her face, only to have it become snagged again.

"I tell you what, wait right here, I got something for that." He dropped her, then turned around and speedwalked toward the kitchen like a person who might have forgotten about a boiling pot on the stove.

Driven purely by impulse, Ruth flung herself out of the open bedroom window with her keys, purse, and phone, tumbling over the window sill and flopping through the gardenia bushes that she had so proudly planted when they first moved into the house. She could hear him bumbling through the house, hollering her name.

When she had managed to lock herself inside of her car, she slid down into the seat and called the police. Her eyes darted across the yard to the windows of the homes that surrounded hers. She waited, barely breathing, for any one of her neighbors' porch lights or bedroom lights to click on. For the slats of someone's window shade to part. For someone to call out into the midnight stillness or come running across the lawn.

Then, only when she was certain that no one had been awakened by the shouting or saw her throwing herself out of the bedroom window—only then did she breathe a sigh of relief.

CHAPTER SIX

When the police arrived, they entered the house and found that he was asleep on the couch. She remained in her car while they walked from one dark room to another, flashlights blazing, dodging the furniture and the personal belongings that Ruth's husband had strewn about in his drunken rage.

Ruth was embarrassed again. Humiliated at having to tell the police that the lights in the house had been turned off, at the neighbors now peering out of their windows, witnessing the drunkard of a husband the police carried from her home.

The two police officers were kind to Ruth, both of them young enough to be her sons. "Ma'am, he could be released as early as tomorrow morning. Maybe there's somewhere that you can go until things cool down between you two? If you are truly concerned for your personal safety, I would suggest that you go to the station tonight and file for an order of protection. That means that he cannot come back to the home or approach you at your place of employment until the order is lifted by the judge."

The second officer handed her a sheet of paper. "Now this is called a victim notification form. It explains your legal rights under the law, and this side," he flipped the sheet over, "lists some information about domestic violence and the contact information for some of our local resources if you need help. Do you have any questions for us?"

Ruth flipped the sheet of paper over in her hands. From the way that the headlights of the police car shone on the paper, the letters on the front and the backside of the sheet seemed to merge together. There was no way she could read it.

"You don't have to arrest him. I don't—I was just hoping that you could kind of talk to him." She was thankful for the darkness that shadowed her face from the young officer.

"I get it. You're afraid of what might happen when he gets out. We see this all the time, and sometimes we can diffuse the situation and let everyone go their separate ways. Unfortunately, in this situation, there is evidence that an assault has taken place and he has communicated a threat of violence, so a mandatory arrest is required. That's the law." He shook his head slowly. "Anyways, ma'am, I would advise you to get on down there and get that order of protection. Just in case."

Like uniformed taxi drivers, the police officers drove away with their belligerent passenger in the backseat— fare compliments of the taxpayers. As Ruth sat in her car and watched them leave, she noticed that the sun was on time for work, and the moon was packing up the darkness, heading home and taking the shadows with it.

She pulled out of the driveway and headed toward the police department. Her car knew these streets well. Knew when to switch from the right lane to the left to avoid the busted asphalt after crossing over the railroad tracks. Knew where traffic would be congested, even at five in the morning, because the school bus drivers would be pulling their clattering, diesel-fueled dinosaurs out of the county bus depot. It knew where the police department was located, even though it drove her straight to the hospital instead.

There were three hours to kill before she would be standing at the computer with Irene again. So much had happened, her mind fought to process it all. Order of Protection. It sounded like something that the President might sign to activate the National Guard. Is that what she needed? And what would happen when it expired? How long did it last?

She had always been a private person, had always made a habit of keeping to herself. She prevented anyone in the community—even her relatives—from knowing what went on inside her house, in her marriage. Now, in a town where she had lived all her life, she was alone. Aimless. Exhausted. She took the elevator to Labor and Delivery, signed in on the sheet and laid on the couch.

She slept a "white" sleep. It was dense and unremarkable, but, no doubt, better than no sleep at all. There were no dreams, no sounds, no consciousness. There was only the ruckus of her heart flopping like a fish out of water in her chest and she was instantly awake.

A notification was flashing on her phone. A text message from Irene: *Where are u? They said the police was at ur house last night.* Followed by another message twelve minutes later:

I told Cynthia that u called out sick, but I saw ur car out there.

Ruth sat on the edge of the couch and tried to collect her thoughts. How had she ended up here? Not here in the on-call room, but here in life. She was grateful to Irene for covering for her, but she couldn't hide here forever. Not even her daughter knew how bad things had gotten.

Two quick knocks on the door and Irene was slipping into the tiny room, closing the door silently behind her. Her hushed whisper called to mind that of a runaway slave on the Underground Railroad.

"I knew you had to be in here somewhere. Are you okay? Honey, they said they saw the police out at your house last night. And honey, I called you but didn't get an answer so, I rode over there, but the house was pitch black. Why didn't you call me if you needed something? Where is he?"

Ruth could have asked who "they", were, but it didn't matter. Instead, she fought to uphold their no-crying-atwork policy and told Irene every unsavory detail of the night's events.

Irene, normally loud and opinionated, was quiet and calm. "So he wanna try to cut somebody, huh? What do you want to do? It's not for me to tell anybody to leave their marriage—I hate to see anyone's family break up—but I want you to know that I support you in whatever you decide to do. You need somewhere to stay? You come on over to my place. You need to borrow some money? I can drive you to the cash advance center." She laughed at her own joke and looped her arm through Ruth's, giving it a sisterly squeeze. "I got you, Boo. You ain't got to live like this. I

KNOW God didn't plan *this* for you." They sat together, quietly for a moment.

"Okay, look here," Irene stood up. "I'll go downstairs and get this hospital rolling and you just take as much time as you need."

At the door, she turned back to Ruth abruptly. "He didn't hurt you, did he?"

Ruth shook her head and tried to smile, hoping to assuage Irene's concerns.

"You didn't hurt HIM, did you?" It had just occurred to Irene that Ruth may well have pulled a Tina Turner on old Ike.

Ruth tried to smile a little harder and shrugged her shoulder.

Irene turned back toward the door and twisted the knob slowly. "Alright, then—I had to ask. See you later, hon."

Chapter Seven

Scientists say that an ant can carry an object that is more than fifty times its own body weight. Ruth remembered that bit of trivia from a science project that she'd helped her daughter with years ago. She wondered if scientists knew that a single sheet of paper was capable of carrying many times more than its own weight, as well. The sheet of paper that she handed to the hospital security guard seemed to be carrying a million times its own weight.

This particular sheet of paper carried all the weight of an official order of protection. It also carried the weight of the unraveled private life that was becoming increasingly difficult for Ruth to conceal. It carried the sense of pride that she had struggled to maintain. It carried the embarrassment, shame, and defeat of her domestic discord. The single slip of paper bore the burden of proof that her personal life was now a matter of public record. And still, it was no match for the weight that remained on Ruth's shoulders—a weight that seemed to increase exponentially as the head of the security team stood there, studying the information on the form.

Tamara had led the hospital's security team for years. She was a large woman in both height and width. At more than six feet tall, every part of her was gigantic. Gigantic hands, gigantic hair, huge rear end, huge bosom, big voice. Her presence commanded attention on any given day, but standing inside the hospital's main entrance in full uniform, there was no questioning who was in charge.

"Well, Ruth," she looked the form over once more before her eyes came back to Ruth. "Well, Ruth, what in the world? I'm sorry. You don't have to tell me anything. I'm not trying to get in your business, but I'll make sure that you don't have any problems while you're here at the hospital. I'll make sure that the rest of the team knows about this," she held the paper up, then placed it on her desk and looked at Ruth apologetically. "What I mean is, I'll make sure that they keep an eye out for him. No one needs to know any other details, so don't worry about that."

Ruth stepped closer to the security station and smiled at Tamara. "I hate to bring my personal life into the workplace, but you know …" she shrugged and searched for a word. "Well, it's life. But I appreciate your help."

Leaning over the desk, Tamara grabbed Ruth's hand. "I'm sorry. I mean, I'm happy if you're happy, if this makes you feel safer. We have a protocol for this sort of thing: the Workplace Domestic Violence Policy. So, we can get you a parking space closer to the entrance or I can have someone walk you out to your car if you ever feel unsafe. And I don't tolerate no stalking, harassment, or threats around here, so don't hesitate to let me know if you need me."

Tamara eased into her chair, leaned back in the seat, and her expression softened. "But I'm sorry that you're dealing with this. My husband never would have put his hand on a woman and he couldn't stand any man who did." A mixture of pride and pain flickered across her face and she paused for the briefest of moments, as though her thoughts had drifted away to a corner of her mind that she didn't visit frequently. It seemed to catch her by surprise.

Ruth was taken aback as well. She had known Tamara for a long time, had grown up in the same town, but their acquaintance had never been anything more than cordial. She hadn't even known that Tamara was married. She might have honestly guessed that Tamara was a lesbian. Maybe it was the masculinity of the security uniform or the fact that Tamara was so much larger than most women, but Ruth was surprised. Equally surprised, both at the unsolicited display of sensitivity *and* the mention of a husband.

She found a small smile. "It's okay. I'm okay. I know everything will work out alright in the end." Turning to leave, she stopped and looked back at Tamara, "You like to read?" Tamara looked up from her desk, confused. "Our book club. We're getting together on the last Thursday of this month. Why don't you join us?"

That night, as Ruth sat in the corner of her patient's room, she prayed that this one was having sweet dreams. Though her lot in life only afforded her the most pathetic quality of sleep, she was always hopeful that her patient was enjoying a beautiful and peaceful sleep—at least while they were on her watch. Sometimes, she tried to will good dreams into existence for her patients if they seemed to be restless or distressed. She'd focus her mind on the image or scenario that she thought would bring her patient the most joy, and she'd concentrate on transferring that thought into the patient's subconsciousness.

She liked to imagine that she had tapped into some form of hypnotherapy or extrasensory perception. No one would probably believe it, but she had seen a few of her patients smile in their sleep on more than one occasion, and she couldn't help but believe that her goodwill method of dream intervention was working.

At the point in the middle of the night when the world was most still, Ruth placed her book in her tote bag and exchanged it for a yogurt cup. Eating was not permitted in the treatment rooms, but she was also not permitted to leave the patient unattended, so if no one was available to relieve her for a break, she sometimes enjoyed a quick snack while things were quiet.

Just as she was fishing around inside her bag for a spoon, Julene peeped into the room and tiptoed inside.

"Miss Ruth, how are you doing? They told me that the police were at your house the other day?" It was both a statement and a question, to which Ruth simply nodded in confirmation and agreement.

"I'm doing well. You know, I'm learning that it's just a part of life. Things have gotten too bad, too much has happened, and it's just best that he and I keep our distance." Unable to locate a spoon anywhere inside her bag, Ruth frowned at the already opened yogurt cup and raised the container to her lips. Yogurt container mid-air, she paused and took note of the fact that Julene was wearing a jacket and purse. "Where you going?"

As if she'd just remembered that her purse was on her arm, Julene reached inside of the bag and produced a sandwich baggie half-filled with plastic spoons. She pulled one spoon from the bag and handed it to Ruth. "The nurses upstairs sent me on a food run." Curving her lips to the side and then turning them down into a frown, she spoke softly. "You're such a nice lady, Miss Ruth. And you're so pretty too. I can't imagine you getting into it with *any*body."

Ruth sculpted her yogurt into the shape of a tiny mountain and resisted the urge to say that everything would be alright. She understood that, as her personal drama transformed into public knowledge, she'd have to learn to accept the pity of the well-intentioned.

Ruth ate her yogurt as Julene continued to speak. "Well, you know what? When enough is enough, you just gotta take care of yourself. My mama used to call it 'self-preservation.' So, you do what you gotta do to make the most out of the rest of your life. If you're getting a divorce, I can refer you to a lawyer. I mean, I have a lot of legal experience, but not in family law or divorce court."

Scooping the last spoonful of yogurt from the cup, Ruth placed the spoon into her mouth and then left it hanging there as she concentrated on peeling small pieces of the foil lid from the edge of the container.

An uncomfortable silence hung in the air.

Julene continued, speaking faster and faster as though she were stumble-running downhill and losing control of her feet. She tried backtracking. "It's not that I'm saying you need a divorce! Or not that you said you want a divorce! Oh Lord, Miss Ruth! Am I saying too much? I mean, I can't even get my kids' father to marry me at all, much less put in the time that your old man did. Who am I to give you advice on this subject? I just want whatever you want. I mean, I'm praying for you and your family. Anything I can do to help … or I can just hush right now …"

She began to back herself out of the room and Ruth stopped her. "Julene, thank you. Sincerely. I know your heart is in the right place." Using the spoon to scrape the bottom corners of the yogurt container, Ruth smiled and cocked her head to look at Julene sideways. "And why do you have a bag full of spoons in your purse?"

A smirk rolled across Julene's face as she glanced inside of her purse. "Lord, my children keep losing my spoons! Every time I go to look for one, they're gone. I don't know what they do when I'm not home, but nobody wants to tell me how they keep disappearing!" She was laughing now, "So I took these plastic ones from the cafeteria and I keep them in my purse so the little munchkins can have something to eat their cereal with."

There was a muffled groan as the person lying in the bed fidgeted around restlessly. The remote control slid off of the bed and dangled over the edge, suspended by the cord. It banged into the bed rails, disturbing the peace. Julene backed out of the room. "Let me get out of here before he wakes up and starts asking for stuff."

Tossing the yogurt cup into the trash, Ruth stood up and hugged Julene. "Thanks for the spoon and everything. And you're right. I need the name of that attorney."

CHAPTER EIGHT

The attorney inhaled deeply, curled her lips together, and exhaled through her nose for a long moment. She looked at Ruth directly and shared a bright smile. When Julene had texted the name of a divorce attorney named Ryan Wilcox, Ruth mistakenly assumed that she'd be sitting down with a white guy to strategize her divorce.

The moment that a young black woman with waist-length dreadlocks and stiletto heels approached her with one hand extended, introducing herself as Ryan, a cocktail of confusion and relief flooded Ruth's body. She preferred to work with a woman, given the subject matter, but she'd never met one named Ryan.

The two women sat together at one end of an overly opulent conference table. Other than the large, swiveling business chairs and a few pieces of abstract art hanging on the walls, the room was empty.

Ryan's voice echoed as she spoke. "Alright, Ruth—we can do this. YOU can do this. We've got some challenges here, but nothing that can't be overcome. Just looking over the information that you've provided," she referred to an itemized checklist that was fastened to the front of a legal file folder, "the major hurdle here is that you'll have to find a new home. It looks like the two of you did build the home together, but it's on heirs' property, which means that it has been passed down through his family and belongs to his family members only. After the divorce, you will no longer have the right to live on that land. Now, without a deed or mortgage on the home, you'll have no rights to that portion of the property either."

"Regarding the—" she paused, taking note of Ruth's broken expression, and laid the legal documents on the table. "Forgive me. I know that this must be very hard for you to digest. Do you need a moment?"

"The house is mine." Ruth barely recognized the small sound of her own voice.

Ryan's expression softened as she adopted an understanding tone. "Divorce is one of the most traumatic experiences that most people will ever endure. That's a fact that you've probably heard before. But what no one tells you is that it's more than just the end of the marriage. It sometimes makes you feel as though you're losing your identity, your lifestyle, your home. But you can begin again. Once the fog clears, you'll see what I mean."

Ruth thought back to the time when her daughter had found a baby turtle in the creek that ran behind the house and how she ruined the carpet when she'd brought the muddy creature into the living room to perform 'first aid.' She remembered the time that she'd hosted the First Lady's luncheon in the dining room and had watched the comedy unfold as the pastor's wife became less and less sanctified with each swig of her mimosa. This house had seen graduation celebrations, summer cookouts, and baby showers. This house had seen some good times. But they hadn't all been good. Ruth's fond reverie dissipated, and she straightened up in her chair. She reminded herself of the scripture that she had read earlier that morning and remembered the feeling of his knuckles pressing into the ridge of her jawbone. Losing the home where she had raised her daughter was bad news, but she'd already guessed as much. It wasn't worse than everything else that she had already lost. She steadied herself and felt the words slip out of her mouth as though they were scripted.

"No, I'm going to be fine. I'm fine. Keep going, please."

The attorney smiled again, a warmer, more encouraging smile, and looked back at the list. "Well, there isn't much marital property, no major assets, no juvenile children or college-aged dependents. I think that it would be pretty easy to separate your debt. You do have an employer-funded retirement account, but I'll request that you be allowed to retain those funds, especially in light of the housing situation, and the judge will make that determination. Unless his attorney fights us on that issue, you should be able to keep it.

"Now, here in the state of Georgia, you are not legally required to live separately for any specific length of time before you can be divorced, and mediation is not required since domestic violence is involved. Once the divorce petition is filed, things should move pretty quickly. We'll assert that the marriage is irretrievably broken, and he'll be served with the documents. That's called the service of process. By law, he has thirty days to file a response, and as long as he doesn't deny that the marriage can't be saved or contest the terms, then the judge can grant an Order of

Dissolution at the end of the thirty days. Any questions about this so far?"

Questions? A stream of questions flooded Ruth's mind. Questions that the attorney couldn't possibly answer. A lifetime together and they had nothing to show for themselves? Getting a divorce, peeling two lives apart, and they didn't even have a piece of furniture that was worth fighting over? "So, basically, I walk away with nothing?" Ryan leaned forward, resting her elbows on the table. "Well sort of. I see this more often than you might think. Lots of folks in our community have built their lives on heirs' property. You know, it's all that some families have to leave to one another. The only kind of legacy or real property. They build their homes on their family's land, brick by brick, and most aren't in the position to approach the banks about taking out a loan for the mortgage."

Ruth nodded, understanding. Understanding and remembering that she and her husband couldn't have qualified for a loan even if they had wanted one. Remembering that her parents had been so eager to get her married off, if for nothing else than to have the freedom to follow their missionary group to third-world countries, winning souls for Jesus.

She recalled that she'd come into the marriage with nothing. No money from her family. No credit. She and her new husband had lived with his mother on the same plot of land where they began building their own home by themselves, paying for the materials and certain portions of the labor as they went along. As they could afford it. Without a bank loan, mortgage, or deed, their home had taken seven years to reach completion. They were living in the back room of her mother-in-law's home when their daughter was born.

The attorney continued. "So, lots of families find themselves in this predicament with no legal or financial documents to show proof of ownership and no assets of tangible value for their children to take with them. But," her voice found a lighter tone, "I'd like to think that you're not walking away with *nothing*. You get to keep your life and you will be safe, and that's more valuable than any material property. Unfortunately, there are too many instances when domestic violence ends in the loss of life. So! Perhaps that's the silver lining in all of this?" She wrapped up her motivational speech and put a smile on it as though she'd placed a bow on a gift. She looked at Ruth, waiting for permission to proceed.

Getting to keep your life wasn't a benefit of divorce, in Ruth's opinion. Shouldn't your life be yours to keep anyway? But she nodded, wanting to end the conversation, knowing that there was no reason to engage the attorney in a discussion on the validity of a custody battle over her own life.

"If you're ready to do this, these are my firm's fees for representation."

Ryan flipped through the file folder and pulled out another itemized sheet, laid it on the desk, and spun it around so that Ruth could read it. A manicured finger slid down the page and pointed to the bottom line.

Sticker shock triggered a frenzy inside Ruth's chest and stole her breath. She swallowed. "Will I be able to make payments on it? I get my direct deposit on the first and the fifteenth. I could probably do about a hundred dollars a month."

Ryan cleared her throat and stood up. "Unfortunately, it's not my firm's policy to enter into financial agreements, but I certainly understand that legal representation during divorce can be costly. As a matter of fact, the cost of the proceedings can sometimes exceed what we've estimated here. So, the sum of these fees represents my retainer, or the amount that I will need up front from you in order to get started. As I work through your case, I'll subtract my hourly rate from the retainer, and if those funds should become depleted before the divorce is finalized, then I can bill you for the additional hours separately."

Freedom certainly wasn't free, Ruth realized, but she was sure that it was worth more than the imitation of life that she was trying to leave behind.

CHAPTER NINE

Irene opened one eye and shot a suspicious look toward Ruth. "What are you standing there snickering about?"

Ruth's laughter burst out of her mouth. "I was just thinking that this must look like some kind of old folks' sleepover. I mean, look at us! It's a geriatric slumber party!"

It was a comical scene that made them both laugh out loud. Irene was laying on her bedroom floor with no makeup and a zebra print satin bonnet on her head. She was flat on her back with her knees bent and her feet planted on the floor so that her red plaid flannel pajama bottoms exposed her ankles. Ruth stood in the doorway wearing a floral caftan that she had purchased from the local dollar store, no bra, hospital slipper socks, and her hair twisted into chunky plaits.

"I know it looks crazy, but this is the only position that makes my back feel better. And sometimes, this doesn't even help. I can't sit, can't stand, it's constant." Irene scooted a little to the left, hoping to find a more comfortable position.

Ruth cocked her head, realizing that Irene's back problems had definitely become worse over the years. "You've always had back problems. As far as I can remember. And you're saying that the doctors can't do anything? Would surgery help?"

Irene winced and groaned while she adjusted herself again, clearly unable to find relief. She stretched her arms out to the sides and twisted at the waist so that her knees were both pointing to the left. She held the stretch for a few moments and tried to control her breathing.

"Doctors don't think surgery would help. They did send me to the physical therapist. That didn't work at all. They keep giving me pills, but you know I don't like taking medication. To tell you the truth, the only relief that I've found is from the chiropractor."

Propping herself up on one elbow to look at Ruth, Irene's frustration became more evident. "I know the doctors don't really think of the chiropractor as a real doctor, but it works! You know Renee from church? The one who helps in the nursery? Don't you remember how she used to use a walker? She had back trouble like me. And then, you remember how Deacon Brison tried to say that he had healed her when he laid hands on her at Bible study last summer? Well, come to find out, she had been going to the chiropractor! Her chiropractor had already straightened her back out to the point where she didn't have to use the walker anymore! That day in Bible study, she didn't even have the walker with her! Came to church without it and Deacon just never noticed." Irene was laughing, barely able to finish the story, "Honey, he's still walking around talking about he got the 'healing hands', trying to touch everybody! Anyway, she gave me the name of the one that she went to, but insurance won't cover it. Everything is out of pocket. So, it's like, which bill won't get paid this month so I can get my back worked on? And

it's not like you can just go one time. You got to keep
going every few weeks until he gets it worked out. That's
seventy or eighty dollars a pop. Honey, I can't afford it!"
She went back to her geriatric floor routine.

That night, Ruth sat on the edge of Irene's sofa. It had
become her bed since leaving her own home via the
bedroom window. The evening after leaving her husband,
she considered checking into a motel, but didn't own a
credit card, and couldn't afford to have a hold placed on
her debit card to cover the expenses. She'd been sitting
in her car, eating a two-piece snack from Church's when
Irene's text message had come through: *I have an extra
room if u need it.*

Irene's mobile home did have a spare room with a
bunk-

bed that her grandchildren used when they slept
over, but Ruth preferred the couch each night. She often
tried to convince herself that sleeping on the couch would
keep her from getting too comfortable or staying too long
at Irene's. That she would have her own place soon. That
the couch helped to make things *feel* temporary because
they *were* temporary. She hadn't admitted, to Irene or to
herself, the bigger reason that the sofa had become her
bed: that she'd become too afraid to sleep in the bedroom
anymore.

Tonight, she knelt to pray before she laid down on the
couch. She prayed for Irene's bad back and the financial
constraints that kept her away from the chiropractor. She

prayed for her own estranged husband who was now an intolerable stranger. Prayed for his health, both physical and emotional. She prayed for Cynthia's speed hump hips, that they would disappear and take the loneliness and insecurity with them. She prayed for the woman underneath, for the husband and children that she seemed to crave so desperately.

She prayed for herself, that she could continue trusting God to guide her through the situations that she didn't understand, that she would be able to afford living alone, that she would have the strength to finally walk away from a bad marriage, that the turbulence in her chest could be quelled for tonight, that she might enjoy the same sweet dreams that she imagined for her sitter-shift patients.

The sweltering heat inside of Irene's small trailer made it impossible to sleep comfortably. Constant clicking and whirring from the tiny window-unit air conditioner was just loud enough to further disrupt Ruth's sleep. Still, the unit's noisy performance was barely adequate enough to elicit a thin stream of cool air which Ruth could only appreciate if she positioned herself right on the edge of the sofa.

When the thin sheet that Irene had draped over the sofa cushions started to creep down into the crack of the couch, and the exposed upholstery began to irritate Ruth's skin, she swung her feet to the floor and sat up in the dark. She listened for a while to the sound of the air conditioner— which now alternated between sloshing water and soft whooshing noises—before she crept into the kitchen to find a snack.

She wasn't exactly hungry, but she stood in front of Irene's refrigerator, holding the door open, hoping to see something that might pique her appetite. A few takeout containers were crammed into the top shelf along with some cans of Ensure and a jug a milk. There was half a bag of grits, a loaf of bread, and something wrapped in crumpled aluminum foil on the middle shelf. The lower shelf held a few snacks that were obviously for her grandchildren—juice boxes, fruit cocktail cups, Lunchables.

A box of Special K cereal was on the shelf on the inside of the refrigerator door. Grabbing the cereal box, the jug of milk, and a bowl, she sat at the kitchen table. Trying to be as quiet as possible so as not to wake Irene, Ruth poured a small mound of cereal into the bowl. It came slowly at first, and then the cereal poured out all at once, spilling out of the bowl and onto the table. A stack of lottery scratch-off tickets slid out of the box and landed atop the cereal pile.

Stunned, both by the cereal avalanche and the hidden lottery tickets, Ruth jumped up, pulled the trash can close to the table and tried to sweep the spilled cereal from the table into the trash bag. She paused occasionally, tipping her ear toward the hallway, straining to listen for any sounds which might indicate that she'd woken Irene. The trailer was dead silent.

Having cleaned up the spilled cereal from the table, she poured half of the flakes from the bowl back into the cereal box and then examined the scratch-off tickets before sliding them back inside the box as well. The string of five tickets were decorated in a way that seemed to make the possibility of winning almost believable. *BUCKS DELUXE! $50,000 TOP PRIZE! WIN $25K FAST! TAXES PAID!* Images of $100 bills covered the tickets and all the spaces on the game pieces had been scratched off, barely revealing the numbers. None of the cards were winners. Apparently, Irene hadn't even bothered to rip the cards apart along the perforated lines. She made a mental note to tease her friend about the odd hiding place and losing tickets in the morning.

When she finished her snack, she crept around the kitchen like a cat burglar, cleaning up after herself, wanting to leave everything exactly as she had found it. Cereal and milk back in the refrigerator. Chair pushed back under the table. *Lion King* placemat wiped clean and straightened. Cereal bowl and spoon rinsed and placed in the dishwasher.

Noting that the dishwasher was full, she searched under the sink for the detergent, filled the dispenser, and pressed Start. The machine started up with more noise than Ruth had anticipated, and she instinctively looked over her shoulder again, hoping that Irene hadn't heard.

Here she was, wanting to be as quiet as possible, but hating the unnatural silence inside of the trailer. When the dishwasher shifted into a quieter gear, Ruth listened harder for some noise. Any noise. The silence seemed to ring in her ears. There should have been something—a passing car, a barking dog, an airplane overhead, the wind blowing. Something. The air conditioner wasn't even whooshing or clicking anymore.

"What are you doing?"

Ruth turned around to see Irene, standing in the partial darkness at the entrance of the kitchen. Her tone was sharp and unfamiliar.

"Nothing. I didn't mean to wake you up. Go on back to bed. I was just starting the dishes, but I'm finished in here now." Ruth moved toward the doorway, only to be pushed back into the kitchen by Irene.

"What did you do? What have you done? Tell me you didn't turn on my dishwasher!" Irene was frantic, down on the floor in front of the washer in an instant, ripping the door open without pressing the stop button.

"You didn't tell me ... you never told me not to use the dishwasher. What's the matter? Is something wrong with it? I wouldn't have ..." Ruth faltered for words as she witnessed Irene's manic behavior.

Water from the dishwasher poured onto the floor and Irene grabbed at the racks that held the dishes inside. The dishes and racks tumbled to the floor, some shattering on impact as they splashed the sudsy water across the room, soaking her nightgown and slipper socks. Unfazed by the broken dishes and puddled water, Irene picked through the mess, collecting wet pieces of paper, handling them gingerly, but unable to prevent them from falling apart in her hands.

"This was my life's savings. This was all that I had." Irene sat in the middle of the floor, bawling, holding handfuls of sopping wet paper as Ruth watched, stunned.

Lottery tickets, scratch-offs, and cash lay limp in Irene's grasp. As Ruth's eyes searched the floor, she saw more cash, more tickets, stuck to the dishes, pasted to the floor, all ruined by the water. Hot bile rose in the back of her throat. *Why had Irene chosen to hide her belongings in the dishwasher? What kind of life's savings was this?*

An intolerable heat rose from Ruth's stomach to her neck and up to her ears. The bizarre scenario left her paralyzed. Irene's scream-crying made her ears ring. There seemed to be a live wire flopping recklessly inside of her chest, and she was awake, sweating feverishly on Irene's couch, body still vibrating from the dream.

Ruth and Irene were standing side-by-side in the sterilization room, wrapping and taping surgical cassettes when Irene's phone rang. Pulling off one glove and using that hand to fish her phone from her cargo pocket, Irene looked at the screen and saw that it was her son.

She stuck the phone between her ear and shoulder and smiled. "What's up, son?" Then, "Honey, hang on. I'mma put you on speaker." She propped the phone up on the shelf in front of the wrapping station and pressed the speaker symbol on the screen. "You there?"

Her son's voice became audible. "What you doing, Ma?"

"Nothing. Me and Ruth sitting on the beach, drinking margaritas." Irene winked at Ruth and nudged her elbow. "Hey, Miss Ruth! It's too early for day-drinking!"

Ruth smiled and continued wrapping cassettes.

"Hi, Nathaniel."

The faint sound of a purring kitten came through the phone. Ruth looked at Irene and raised a questioning eyebrow. Irene leaned closer to the phone. "Is that a cat I hear in the background?"

"Yeah, I got a sphynx."

Irene shot another look at Ruth, confused, and spoke toward the phone. "What is that? Like a hairless cat?"

"Yeah, a hairless cat. Her name is Stella. She's crying like a little baby 'cause she wants me to pick her up. She's spoiled." Nathaniel was muttering baby talk to the kitten, apparently holding her now.

"What made you get a cat?"

"Oh. I had to go to South Carolina to get this cat. They don't have these around here. It was $1,000 dollars."

"Son, but how did *you* get it? You bought it?"

"Well we split it. Me and Dee-Dee."

Irene rolled her eyes toward Ruth. She guessed that her son was back on good terms with his daughter's mother. "So, what is this? Are you two co-parenting now? Y'all can barely agree when it comes to Kenzie and now you're buying animals together?"

"Heck no! We just did it because of a business situation. Because, like, if Stella has three or four litters, each kitten is worth like $1,200."

"But who does it mate with?"

"Uh, any sphynx. Well, we would pay them like $300 or $400 or give them one of the kittens. And we just mate them. We can find one around here or we can go online and find one. But she hasn't even had her first heat cycle yet, so we're just waiting."

Ruth disappeared into the supply closet for more sterilization wrap and took her place next to Irene again. Nathaniel's ambitious business plan continued to unfold.

"… starts having kittens, it will be like $1,200 per cat." Irene was struggling to get a new roll of sterilization tape into the holder, only half-listening. "Wow. Do you know anyone else who has one?"

"No, but I know a lot of people who want one now that they see ours. Because it's rare to see one. Oh, and we have Rari too. He's a pit. His name is short for Ferrari."

Irene, annoyed, both with the tape holder and the conversation, switched places with Ruth. "Nathan! What are you talking about? You got a pit bull too?"

"Yeah basically. But he's at her place most of the time. The cat is with me most of the time, but sometimes I have the dog too. I like the cat more than the dog. Really, I just like the money part. And she's so elegant. She has light blue eyes. She's a cute cat. Remember when I used to watch *Aristocats* when I was little? I had never seen one in real life until now."

Clearly irritated with the subject, Irene closed her eyes and took a deep breath before speaking toward the phone again. "There was no sphynx in that movie. It was a Siamese cat. Besides, that isn't important right now. Did you enroll in any classes at the community college for this semester?"

"No, I'm just working this summer and then I'm going to try and get into the IT program. That's my new major. I was looking at jobs and they got a bunch of IT jobs out there."

Ruth's heart went out to Irene. She'd had these same, bewildering conversations with her own daughter. The kids were all over the place with these random ideas. One minute they wanted to get rich breeding animals, the next they were jumping from one college course to another, hoping that a degree would fall into their laps and make them wealthy overnight.

Preferring to discuss education rather than animal-breeding, Irene replied, "Yeah, I guess with the banks and some of these big businesses out here, I'm sure there are good jobs in technology."

"Yeah, I looked at one job at this place called ITAA CRAFF? Or something like that."

"Okay, that's TIAA/CREF. They handle financial services like investments, insurance, and retirement funds. Yeah, one of the surgeons here at the hospital, his wife is in the Human Resources department over there."

"They started my boy out with $73,000! Shoot! You think she can help me?"

"Yeah, I can talk to her and find out what you need to do. And she's a real smart sister. She's a Delta, so she's smart." Irene glanced over at Ruth and shrugged her shoulders, unsure about the accuracy of her last statement, guessing that it sounded plausible.

Nathaniel had no problem accepting this as fact. "Yeah, I know she got connections. That's so cool, you know. Because that's how you get in. Usually, the people with the resumes don't get in. That's what people keep telling me."

"Knowing someone definitely helps. Anyone can go to college and get a degree, so that means, after college, everyone is starting from the same place. You have to either know somebody, or get an internship, or have some kind of qualifications to make yourself stand out. It's going to have to be more than a degree and it's going to take more than a few good grades. You're going to have to work for it." She didn't want to discourage him but needed to get him to take things seriously. "IT is such a huge field and there's so much competition ..."

Undeterred, a bit of excitement peppered Nathaniel's voice and he was on a roll. "I want to be either a mobile device developer or something like that. I was looking at some stuff yesterday. There's a lot of good companies to work for."

Hoping that her son would finally act on his big ideas, Irene tried to sound encouraging. "Well, that's good. Keep feeling around this summer, look for some internships, and look for some jobs this summer that are related to what you want to do, just so you can get a taste of it."

"Okay. I'mma do that. I need those internships for real."

Irene continued, "Even hospitals and health care companies are needing computer people. I know, at our hospital, they are having to go paperless, and they're trying to do marketing, but their big problem is with online security and protecting everyone's information. All I keep hearing is 'secured this' and 'encrypted that.' It sounds like this cyber safety stuff is a big deal. So, you just need to find what you like and what will be making you money in the future. You're gonna have to get in where you fit in."

"Okay. I need to start looking for real now." His voice was sounding more serious, more mature than the boy who had just been talking about breeding cats.

"Alright, well start now. I don't care if you get a job at the Car Stereo Warehouse, or if you're doing TV installation and surround sound. You know how to hook all that equipment up. I've seen you with that Playbox thing and those speakers in that back room! Everything is going to computers these days! I saw a commercial for a smart mattress the other day! Can you believe that? Some kind of iMattress!"

Nathaniel chuckled about the iMattress, but turned serious again. "I know! See, the only thing is, I'm trying to get some certifications this year. This dude I know at the cellphone place, he was going to hire me there for a good job, but he said I have to get these certifications first."

"Alright! Is it something you can take online? Or at the community college on a weekend?" Irene looked around for Ruth and, seeing that she had finished wrapping the last of the cassettes and was now loading them into the autoclave, made eye contact with her and mouthed the word *'Sorry'* before turning back toward the dirty side to refill the ultrasonic tank for the next load of instruments.

Nathaniel continued, "It's something I can do online, but it's so expensive. It's almost $1,000 dollars. I can probably get it for free at school once I get into the IT program. It's probably a class I'll have to take anyway. 'Cause you get all the certifications when you're in the program. But I want it now so I can start working."

Ruth stopped loading the autoclave and whipped her head toward Irene, knowing full well what she would have said, had she been having this conversation with her own child. Irene held a blue-gloved hand up toward Ruth and mouthed *'I got it.'* Ruth grinned and mouthed back, *'My bad. Handle your business.'*

Irene moved closer to the phone and steadied her voice. "Now son, let me say this. And I hope and pray that you take this with love, 'cause you know I love you, but I want you to think about what you said. You just spent almost a thousand dollars on a durn cat."

Nathaniel began to backpedal with the expertise of a seasoned congressional candidate. "OH! I didn't. I only spent like, three, maybe four hundred. My homeboy paid the rest."

Ruth and Irene smirked knowingly at one another. Irene, ignoring the blatant lie, tried to make her point. "Okay, but you could have invested that into yourself. Just the way that you and Dee-Dee or your homeboy or *whoever* can invest in a cat that *might* make you some money, you can invest that money in these courses and classes you need to take!"

She tried to control her voice, to avoid yelling. She was glad that he was even talking about his plans with her at all. It was rare to get this much conversation out of him. "Even if that class is $1,000 and you only have $400, we can put in a couple hundred to help you out, just have that passion and invest in yourself like that." There was no response.

Ruth came over and gently pushed Irene away from the sink so that she could finish filling the ultrasonic tank with water. Irene bit the corner of her lower lip and spoke gently into the phone. "You know, I do the same thing. I'll say something is expensive, like a doctor's bill or something, but then I'll go spend $40 on some Mary Kay makeup or a pedicure."

Nathaniel's voice returned to the phone. "Yeah, you're right! I'm the same way! It's expensive unless you want it. If you want it, you always figure out how to pay for it."

Irene sighed, relieved that her lecture hadn't caused her baby boy to shut her out. "Well, son, just get your hands on something. Some kind of job. Just try something. You don't want to spend four or five years in college and find out you don't like the job. And let me tell you something, they are teaching some of this stuff to the kids at the elementary school already. You know Kenzie is doing her homework on that website called Khan Academy, and the other day she was playing some little game on there that teaches little girls how to write computer codes! I sat right there and watched her build a little app where she had the character running and jumping and everything! And it was free! Now, don't let your baby outdo you!"

Nathaniel was laughing at the thought of his own daughter being smarter than him. "Ma, that girl is a trip! I'mma look into that though." He was quiet for a moment, then, "Mama! You want to know what I really want to do with my life?"

"Talk to me, son." Irene was working to tie up the over-

filled biohazard bag under the counter.

"I want to start a business."

Gingerly standing up from her stooped position under the counter, Irene looked at Ruth, rolled her eyes, and pretended to faint.

"Look boy, you have access to everything that you need, for whatever you want to do! Use your resources, most of it is free! Probably ninety percent of what you learn will come from outside of the classroom. Information is FREE! If you know the owners of that cellphone company or anyone else, you need to stick close to them, make friends with them, talk to them as much as you can, even try to move up within their business if you can. You can be a manager. Stick with them. They can teach you a lot, and not just what works, but they can also tell you what didn't work, or what they wish they did different, or what obstacles they ran into. Learn from them, use them, or get on that computer and learn some stuff for yourself! Stop talking about it and pick something and just do it!"

"Dang, Mama! Listen to you dropping all of this wisdom! You too smart to still be working in that old sterilization room!"

"Ouch! That hurt, son! But okay, maybe you can do better than I did. You got the same number of hours in your day as all of those rappers you always listen to! What are their names? Drake? The Three Amigos? Use your time! What's stopping you?" Irene looked toward Ruth and shrugged her shoulders, eyes begging for help with the rap names. Ruth laughed as she shrugged back.

"Alright, alright, Mama. I know! I'mma handle mine, don't worry. I gotta go anyway."

"Okay, son, give me a call later."

"Right, Mama. And it's the *Migos*. Not the Three Amigos!" He was still laughing when he ended the call.

Sliding the phone back into her pants' pocket, Irene looked at Ruth and shook her head. As she pushed a new biohazard bag into the receptacle, Ruth spoke first. "I can't help you with the rap names."

Irene pushed the receptacle back under the cabinet, stood and looked at Ruth for a long minute.

"What?"

Irene leaned against the counter and exhaled heavily. "I just don't understand my boy. I raised him the best that I could. Kept him in church, Bible study, vacation Bible school. Gave him plenty of books. He's smart! But he has no direction! He's all over the place. I just want him to get a job. Isn't that what people used to do? Graduate, get a job, work, and pay your own bills until you retire? What happened to this generation?"

Ruth leaned against the counter next to Irene and nodded her head. "I don't know. I feel like I have the same conversations with mine. She changes her mind more than anyone I know! Just called me the other day and asked me to Western Union her some money so she could take a class to learn how to do fake eyelashes! I just paid for her to get into some kind of business where you go to people's houses to do lingerie parties. I told her don't call me asking for another dime!"

Irene side-eyed Ruth, lips twisted to the side. "You gave it to her, didn't you?"

Ruth was silent, her expression sheepish. "Look, this conversation isn't about me! Let's get these cases caught up before lunch."

CHAPTER TEN

After lunch, Ruth headed toward Cynthia's office. The moment that she stepped into the room, she thought about turning around to leave. Cynthia was sitting at her desk, dabbing the corners of her eyes with a tissue, apparently too overcome with tears to finish unpacking her lunch. Jenny Craig pre-packaged meals, some fruit cups, and large jug of water were spread out on the desk in front of her. Ruth paused at the doorway, wanting to back away, but she'd already been spotted.

It wasn't that she didn't have compassion for whatever was causing Cynthia so much distress, but she'd always felt so awkward about invading anyone else's privacy— especially when they were upset. She'd grown up in a small, proud family, where weaknesses and vulnerabilities belonged behind closed doors.

But Cynthia wasn't just a casual stranger. She was a church member, a book club friend, a work friend.

"You okay?" She asked the question as gingerly as possible, giving Cynthia the option of privacy or transparency— whichever she preferred. Cynthia looked down at her hands where the tissue had been reduced to a soggy pile of mono-colored confetti. Tears streamed down her face and disappeared under her chin, reappearing as fat raindrops on her chest.

"I. Am. So. Tired. Ruth." She was choking now, forced to alternate between breathing and speaking clearly. "My mama. Ruth, I'm doing my best to take care of her, but she makes it so hard. The home health nurse quit. Said she couldn't work in an abusive environment. Mama acts up so bad when the people come to the house. I'm the only one who can do anything for her! And I'm there every day!"

She dumped the pile of shredded tissue into the trash can under her desk and continued. "I mean, obviously, the stroke wasn't her fault. But she isn't mentally impaired. She doesn't have dementia! She's just so mean, so bossy and rude! So, she's saying that the aides have been stealing from her and now they won't come to the house anymore unless someone else is there."

Ruth nodded, beginning to understand the complexity of the situation. Cynthia tried to regain control of her breathing. "So, I'm at her house all of the time now. Sometimes she treats me like I'm the home health aide, and other times she acts like I'm her wife! I'm her housekeeper! I'm her hired companion! The only break I get is when I'm at work, and it's so exhausting."

She was speaking faster now, anger overtaking the tears, and she spoke as though she had never been afforded the opportunity to express her feelings out loud. "I can't do anything for myself. At my last physical, the doctor said that my blood pressure was up, and I had gained thirty pounds. They wanted to put me on medication, but they said that I could probably get it under control with diet and exercise. Problem is, I'm too stressed to eat right or workout because I'm trying to take care of *her*!"

Ruth thought it over, understanding the sacrifices that come with caring for an aging parent. The responsibility requires some hard decisions. "What about assisted living or a nursing home for her?"

Cynthia shook her head slowly. "She was in a skilled nursing facility for a while, but Medicare only pays for the first hundred days of care. I tried to get her on Medicaid, but she doesn't qualify. By law, she can't have more than $2,000 in assets. And then, even if they pay, she still needs money for her glasses, clothes, dental care—you know, all of her personal expenses—but she can't afford those things if she only has $2,000 in assets. The system is set up so that, if you qualify for Medicaid, and they pay for you to be in a facility, then all of your income goes to the facility moving forward. So, her social security and pension and everything will go to the nursing home!

"And, honestly, I feel so guilty about putting her in one of those places when the doctors are saying that she's still able to live in her own home. She wants to live out the rest of her life in the house that she built with my daddy. So, now she feels like I should give up my apartment and move in with her since I'm not married. I mean, I guess it makes sense, but …" Her voice trailed off, the sentence falling into the treacherous gap between a mother's guilt trip and a daughter's right to life.

The situation was a logistical and moral nightmare, and the weight of that reality caused both women to fall silent. Ruth tried to imagine herself in twenty or thirty years. How would she care for herself? What would she ask of her daughter? What would her daughter be willing to do for her? Her daughter loved her. All daughters love their mothers. But words like responsible, organized, and dependable weren't the most accurate descriptors for her only child. The idea of placing her own well-being into her daughter's hands disturbed her.

In the silence, Cynthia found the courage to confess the root of her frustrations. "And I'm young, Ruth! Not as young as I was, but I can still have children. I still want a husband." She broke down again, sobbing inconsolably. "But I don't even have time to take care of myself! The doctor gave me a pamphlet called *Self-Care for the Caregiver.* Do you think that my mother would let me spend time on self-care when I could be pampering her? I swear, if I didn't know better, I would think that she's jealous of me paying attention to anyone besides her— even myself!

"When I try to go to the gym, she has a crisis, she's in pain, she needs me to do something for her. When I try to eat healthy, she wants meatloaf, spaghetti, mashed potatoes. And I love that stuff, obviously ..." she looked down at her stomach and thighs and sighed heavily. "I don't have much willpower as it is. I mean, pizza, cake, if she eats it, I'm eating it too. I'm eating ALL of it! So, it's like she loves to see me eat. Like she wants to keep me fat and single and trapped in the house with her forever."

Ruth, sensing Cynthia's need to vent, stood quietly as she continued.

"I know it's wrong, the way I feel and the way she treats me. I just keep wondering what I did to make my life turn out like this? I'm a good person, Ruth! I work hard. I love the Lord. I just keep asking why hasn't He placed me in someone's heart yet? When do I get *my* turn?"

She had covered the edges of her desk calendar with curlicues and other doodles as she spoke, but she stopped mid-swirl and looked up at Ruth, embarrassed by her own rambling. "Oh Lord, Ruth, I am so sorry! I just dumped my whole life story on you, and that's not what you came for. What's up? Are the surgical assistants sneaking down to sterilization and taking instruments off of the case carts again? Because I—"

"Well, um …" Ruth searched for the words that she had rehearsed in her mind last night as she lay on Irene's couch, waiting for sleep to come.

"Puh-leeze don't tell me you're about to quit!" Cynthia leaned back in her chair, hand over her heart.

"No, that's not it. I couldn't afford to quit anyway. No, I need to withdraw some money from my 401(k). I have some attorney's fees to pay and I'm putting a deposit on a trailer. I'm getting a divorce." She hadn't planned on divulging so much information. Inside, she was as shocked at herself as Cynthia apparently was.

Cynthia's face dropped. She leaned across the desk and grabbed Ruth's hand. "Oh my God, Ruth. I'm sorry. I didn't know! I mean, I admit, I had heard that there were some problems. But I'm not married, and I don't have any experience in that department, so I kept my mouth closed. How are you holding up? Do you need anything? What can I do?"

"There you go, always the caregiver." Ruth smiled and squeezed her hand. "I'm fine. You have enough on your plate. What do they always say? The Lord hasn't brought me this far to leave me now. I'm trusting Him. I just hate that I have to dig into my little bitty retirement fund for this. On the other hand, I should consider it a blessing. At least I can afford to leave. Even if it's only just barely."

"To God be the glory!" Cynthia sat back in her chair again. "I'll get the forms in for you today, and here," she dug down in her purse and pulled out a thin strip of paper. "Here, this was in my fortune cookie last night. Mama wanted Chinese," she made a face, "but I think this message was meant for you."

She pressed the paper into Ruth's hand and stood to hug her. They laughed. "Look at us! Too much emotion for one day!" Ruth pulled away, stepped back, and exhaled while she fanned her face with her hand.

Stepping out of Cynthia's office, she came face to face with an amused-looking Irene. "Everything okay? You two looked like you were in the middle of some kind of love fest, so I didn't want to interrupt." She looped her arm through Ruth's and walked with her back into the sterilization area. "Don't let me find out that someone's gunning for my spot as Number-one Best Friend?" She grabbed Ruth's hand and patted the back of it, making an exaggerated sad face. "What did she give you? You know I was eavesdropping. Not being nosey, you know that's not me!" Irene was laughing now. "I was just listening in case I had to run in there and rescue you!"

Ruth reached into her pocket and pulled the slip of paper out so that they could both see it. She looked at Irene. "You've got your glasses on, read it for me!"

Irene took the paper and held it almost at arm's length. "It says, *'You never know how strong you are until strong is your only choice.'*—*Bob Marley.*"

CHAPTER ELEVEN

What kind of outfit is appropriate for the day that you go to court and stand before the judge to ask for your freedom papers? Today, she had to work, and she'd taken a long lunch so that she could go get divorced. Today she wore scrubs.

This morning, Irene had commented that she seemed so unemotional, and Ruth suspected that this was true. Perhaps it was the way that she'd been raised and the way that she'd always been. To take care of business now and feel all the feelings later, at a more convenient time. Today, that was the defense mechanism that prevented her from falling apart as she left work, drove to the courthouse, and stood outside the courtroom, waiting for her attorney.

"Hey, Ruth! How are you feeling? Nervous? Don't be." Ryan Wilcox floated toward her as though they were just a couple of girlfriends getting together for coffee. Shaking Ruth's hand, Ryan didn't even wait for a response, just lowered her voice and leaned in toward Ruth's ear. "He's in there, I checked. But he doesn't have an attorney. Now, here's what's going to happen: We'll present your written and signed agreement, and the judge will ask you both some simple questions. You know, like, do you want a divorce today? Where and when did you get married? Are there any personal or real estate property rights to be decided?

We've been over this. Nothing has changed. These are formalities, okay?"

Ruth, realizing that she was still shaking Ryan's hand, let her hand relax a little bit in Ryan's grip and nodded her head.

Ryan had the strategic energy and focus of a coach prepping a boxer before a big match. "We've included all of the required and pertinent information in your packet, including your request to retain your retirement fund. He's received a copy of the documents as well. As long as he confirms that he is not contesting the terms of the agreement, then the judge will sign the decree and it's a done deal!"

Ryan held up her hands to simulate the dropping of the mic and Ruth couldn't help but feel as though her attorney had just given her a tutorial on how to download apps on her cellphone. Easy peasy. The routine-ness of the process was more impersonal than it appeared on TV and, for some reason, that fact both comforted and irritated Ruth.

Walking back to her car, she checked the time. Twenty-six minutes. That's how long it had taken to cut her losses and he hadn't tried to fight it at all. Probably hadn't even read through the details of the agreement, knowing him. She sat in her car, trying to get her mind around it. She was divorced. What did it feel like? She'd thought about this moment from the day that she'd first stepped into Ryan's office. Thought about whether she'd feel sad. Wondered if she might feel happy. Sitting in the car, she just … didn't.

Back at work, feeling numbness if anything, she opened her locker to find a paperback book which was adorned with a handwritten note and a green Christmas bow. She stood rooted to the spot for a moment, reading and re-reading the title, *Single, Married, Separated, and Life after Divorce*. The note, written in Irene's elegant cursive penmanship, read:

> *"For I know the plans I have for you,'*
> *declares the Lord, 'plans to prosper you*
> *and not to harm you, plans to give you*
> *hope and a future (Jeremiah 29:11)."*
>
> *This helped me, hope it helps you.*
>
> *Love you for life,*
> *Your friend, Irene*

Sitting down on the breakroom bench and leaning forward to rest her elbows on her knees, Ruth studied the pattern of the tiles on the floor. The state of unfeelingness was frightening. She thought about the last question that the judge has asked her today: *"Do you agree to the terms and conditions of the marital settlement agreement set forth in front of you here today? Please answer 'I do.'"* What kind of irony was that? The same two words—*I do*—that had been required to join them together were the same two words that were required to rip them asunder.

Without warning, tears began to sprinkle the floor, one after another, until the tiles seemed to swim and drift out of position. Fat droplets that didn't feel like they had even taken the time to well up in her eyes as normal tears might, but instead just fell straight from her eyes to the floor.

She sat motionless and let them fall, lacking the energy to stop them. After a while—she couldn't be sure if two minutes had passed or twenty—Irene's leopard print clogs appeared in Ruth's peripheral view, moved across the tile floor, and stopped next to the bench where Ruth was sitting. There was a hand on her shoulder, squeezing for a moment in the silence, and then the clogs moved into the periphery again, disappearing from view.

CHAPTER TWELVE

The home that Cynthia and her mother now shared was a caricature of their new, blended life. The white aluminum screen door with scalloped edges opened into a pristine front room with a low ceiling, plastic-covered couches, and plastic flowers. The pictures of Martin Luther King, Jr. and John F. Kennedy thumb-tacked to the walls showed that this was a home that had obviously been the pride and joy of an old-school, African-American mother from another generation.

Now, the home was run by a modern, single woman who clearly had a weakness for Target and Pinterest. The clash between the civil rights decor and the shabby chic furnishings was immediately noticeable. Compared to the front room, the den and dining rooms could have easily belonged to a completely different home. These two rooms were filled with white-washed, weathered furniture, distressed aluminum pails cradling miniature succulents, and plush neutral throws draped casually over the arms of the chairs. Antique books and suitcases were stylishly arranged in a corner. The dining room featured a rustic shiplap wall and a reclaimed crystal chandelier. Both rooms were accented with deliberately placed mason jars, antique milk jugs, pillows, candles, and vintage graphic art.

For tonight's book club meeting, Cynthia chose a Mediterranean theme. In presentation alone, she had outdone herself. She enjoyed losing herself in the creativity of event planning and welcomed the opportunity to show off her domestic skills. One day, she would be the kind of wife who hosted events like this for her girlfriends while her husband was away on a golf outing or a business trip.

She could hear Irene's voice even before the doorbell rang: "I don't feel right about coming over to somebody's house and bringing NOTHING!" She heard Julene's voice responding: "Right, but you're supposed to bring a hostess gift. Like a bottle of wine or a candle or something."

"I wasn't raised to bring no wine and candles! That's why I brought this macaroni and cheese. That's what I always bring, so don't be trying to change things now."

When Cynthia unlatched the screen door to let them in, Irene was standing there, holding an enormous aluminum casserole pan covered in a thick layer of aluminum foil, all wrapped in a red kitchen towel. "Where you want me to put this?" Then, pointing toward Julene with her elbow, she stage-whispered, "First time here and already trying to tell *me* what to do!"

Cynthia laughed as the rest of the ladies filed in through the front room behind Irene and the macaroni, greeting each other with hugs and air kisses, politely complimenting Cynthia on her mother's home. When they rounded the corner into the dining room, they were speechless, stunned by the professionally displayed food and the expertly coordinated decor.

The women walked around the table, taking in the beautiful food and thoughtful details. There were petite chicken and shrimp kabobs, a platter of turkey pitas topped with fresh slaw, pasta salad in a footed serving bowl, a bowl of hummus on top of a three-tiered serving platter with triangles of pita bread and sliced cucumbers arranged on the lower tiers, and fresh fruit with creamy fruit dip in colorful ramekins. On the end of the table, a vintage glass beverage pitcher held homemade limeade with slices of lime floating on top. Next to the pitcher, a beverage tray lined with a lace cloth held margarita glasses rimmed in teal, pink, and yellow sugar crystals. Each dish was accented with a tiny toothpick flag which listed the names of the various Mediterranean inspired delicacies.

Irene stood holding the baked macaroni wrapped in the greasy towel. "I don't even want to put this on your pretty table! You should have told us it was being catered."

Cynthia smiled, flattered by the compliment. "It's not catered. I did this! I wanted to surprise you all with something a little more sophisticated. Plus, I'm trying to get this off of me," she put her hand on her hip and turned sideways so everyone could see her rear. "I'm trying to do better. Trying to get me a man!" She took the casserole from Irene and placed it on the table, "But ain't NO WAY that we can let this good macaroni go to waste! Y'all, I'm trying to eat better, but I can't pass up baked macaroni. I guess God ain't through with me yet! Okay, come on now! Who's going to bless the food? Ruth? Irene?"

The ladies gathered in the dining room, circled around the table and joined hands, heads bowed. Irene, departing from her normally comedic demeanor, adopted a more serious tone:

"Lord, Father, God … Thank you. Lord, we come to thank you tonight for all you've done. Lord, you just keep on blessing us, even when we don't deserve it, God."

The room vibrated with the soft sounds of jangling earrings and bangle bracelets as the women squeezed each other's hands and murmured in agreement.

Irene continued, *"God, only you can supply all of our needs. And you are fair, Lord, by making a way for the haves and the have-nots, and—"* stifled giggles floated around the circle, and Irene opened a single eye to shoot a stern look around the group before resuming her prayer. *"And Lord God, thank you for bringing our group together, that we made it to this place safely, that our circle is yet unbroken but continues to grow. We know that we are not here by accident, but by your divine will, so we thank you for your wisdom and grace. And thank you for the food that has been prepared, for the hands that prepared it, that it may be the nourishment that we so need for our bodies."*

Murmurs and "Yes, Lord, thank you, Lords" became increasingly audible.

"In your precious son Jesus' holy name, amen." The room breathed a collective "amen."

When everyone had settled into the den to eat and mingle, Cynthia began to get the meeting under way. She stood in front of the ladies, holding a beaten notebook. "So, this is Irene's birth month, but before we get to the fun part, let's make sure that everyone has been properly introduced." She looked at Ruth: "Thank you for inviting two guests. That makes twelve of us!" There was a small round of applause. "Ladies," she motioned toward Julene and Tamara, "would you stand and introduce yourselves?"

Julene stood up, waved at the group, "Well, most of y'all know me from work. I'm Julene. I'm a CNA but I'm working on getting my RN. Before this, I was a paralegal." She paused and smiled. "I got a little bit of legal knowledge if anybody needs me! Oh! And I have three little blessings, but they're at home with their daddy. Miss Ruth invited me here because I begged her to rescue me from the snotty noses and the dirty diapers—the ones at home *and* at work!" She laughed and sat down, clearly entertained by her own joke.

Tamara stood up next. "Most of you probably know me already from work too. But, for those who don't, I'm hospital security. Don't nothing happen down there that gets past me!" She laughed. "That last part was just a joke. I'm sure there have been one or two nurses and maintenance guys meeting up in some supply closet when I'm not looking! Hope it's none of you all." Someone in the room coughed and a few people laughed out loud.

Tapping her lower lip with her index finger, Tamara thought for a moment. "Um, what else? Well, I got married and became a widow in the last six months, so that's been crazy."

Ruth was floored. "You just mentioned your husband to me the other day for the first time!"

Tamara's shoulders slumped. For such a large woman, she suddenly looked fragile and vulnerable. "Yeah, y'all. Let me tell you something about life." She shook her head slowly, not exactly sure what she wanted to tell anyone about life. "Well, back in high school I used to date William Dudley. He was from around here. You might have known him as Liam or Lee. Anyways, he was ahead of me in school and he went off to the military after he graduated. I was still in school, so we basically broke up when he left. Can't keep no long-distance relationship going when you're that young!" She paused, a small smile floated across her face as she remembered their young and foolish days.

"Okay, so fast-forward, we went our separate ways. He married some girl from overseas, I had a baby by James Dixon and ended up marrying him. I didn't even really like James! You know what they say about a marriage of convenience." She rolled her eyes. "Well, I always thought about William over the years. I heard he had gotten married and was living up in Ohio or somewhere but I could not figure out how to get in touch with him. His family moved away from here and he wasn't on any social media sites. By then, I was divorced from The Jerk, thank the Good Lord. Later, I found out that William had been thinking about me too, and when his wife died from cancer, he tried to look me up. Come to find out, he had looked in one of our old alumni directories that hadn't been updated in years, and it said that I was married— which I wasn't anymore!—so he didn't reach out to me.

"Then, probably three or four years after that, I took a chance and looked him up online again. I found his name listed on his wife's obituary. His contact information was on it, so I called him and we reconnected. It was so nice to talk to him again!"

The room was dead silent. Every woman sat motionless,

completely enthralled with Tamara's story.

"Well, first it was just the phone calls. Phone calls turned into long weekends together, and long weekends became vacations. I mean, we were high school sweethearts and he was still the same great guy. So, after about a year and a half of the long-distance thing, he decided to move down here.

"We bought a cute house, and you know, he's good with the handyman stuff, so even though it needed a lot of work he was taking his time doing most of it himself. Then his leg started hurting and we figured that he had strained it doing all of that renovation work, so we tried ibuprofen and heat packs and everything. Nothing worked. Went to the doctor, the doctor referred him to the orthopedist. Went to the orthopedic surgeon and they did a scan of his leg and sent us straight to the oncologist."

The women in the room were shaking their heads in disbelief, unable to reconcile the rapid downturn of events. A box of tissues made its way around the room. The sound of the Judge Mathis Show, coming from somewhere in the rear of the house, suddenly seemed inappropriately loud.

Tamara fumbled with the cuffed sleeve of her denim jacket, and her story continued. "Come to find out, he had lung cancer. He did smoke years ago when he was in the service—everybody did—but he quit at least twenty years ago. He told me he had been coughing some stuff up, but he didn't really think much of it. Well, the cancer had already spread through his entire body, all down his leg and so that's what was causing the leg pain. The orthopedic surgeon said they see this all the time. So, y'all, literally within a month, just thirty days, he was dead. He was in the oncology facility down the road and there was nothing they could do for him. The day before he died, he said he was feeling a little better, and our plan was to get married anyway, so the nurses threw us a wedding."

She didn't cry, but the tears were in her voice. She was still grieving. Still trying to comprehend. Some of the women in the room were dabbing the corners of their eyes with tissue.

"I'm telling you! These nurses." Tamara was nodding her head, visibly humbled. "They got flowers, got the minister to stay after work, the registrar came down to the hospital after hours to do the marriage license. And we got married right there in his room. And the next day he was gone. He didn't even have life insurance."

A pair of tears ran down her face as gracefully as synchronized swimmers. She used her jacket sleeve to wipe her cheeks, her chin. "But, you know what? I still trust God. I miss my friend, Lord knows I do, but if I didn't have my faith …" she shook her head slowly again, voice trailing off. No words.

Tamara looked around at the ladies in the room as though she had been awakened after accidentally nodding off to sleep. Wiped her face again. Smiled. "So. That's me. That's my story."

Ruth walked over and hugged her tightly. "I am so sorry.

I had no idea. And I remember old Liam. Old Will-Lee-

Yum! I didn't even know he had moved back here."

Other ladies were getting up, gathering around, offering their condolences, sharing stories about who knew whom and who had known Liam back in the day.

Tamara cleared her throat. "Okay! If we don't change the subject, we're all just gonna sit here and cry our eyes out, so Cynthia, carry on. I know my story must sound like some kind of Lifetime original movie. Sorry if I depressed everyone."

Cynthia took center stage again. "Whew! Okay! Tamara, for real, if you need something, anything, let us know. We got you." When everyone had taken a seat, Cynthia took an envelope out of her dog-eared notebook and asked for a drum roll, please. In the crescendo, she made the announcement: "To our guest of honor, Miss Irene Arnold, happy birthday!"

She handed the envelope to Irene, who ripped it open and held the ten crisp $100 bills up in the air. "Take a picture of it, y'all, because it will probably be gone by tomorrow."

Amid the laughter and jokes, the women hadn't noticed when Julene's facial expression transformed from lighthearted to stone-faced, as though someone had flipped a switch. They did notice, however, when she stood up abruptly and stormed toward the door, cutting across the room with no apologies for the interruption. They fell silent, confused by the behavior of the young woman who'd seemed so comfortable and happy just moments before.

Julene paced back and forth in the doorway of the living room threatening to leave but wanting answers first. Other than the rhythmic melodies of *Mediterranean Nights* floating in the background, her voice was the only sound in the room. Each of the ladies sat frozen in place, with varying facial expressions that hovered between shock and amusement. "Okay." Julene pressed her thumb and forefinger against her forehead, the other fingers splayed out like a handful of exclamation points. "Okay, hold up. Hold up, hold up, hold up!" She was speaking in tongues, the disbelief reducing her vocabulary to gibberish. "So, THIS is what y'all do?" She shot a look that sliced through the room. No one moved.

"So, y'all are just gonna hand this lady—" she pointed a finger at Irene so there would be no mistaking to whom she was referring. "Y'all just gonna hand her $1,000 CASH? And act like it ain't NOTHIN'?" She sounded like she was scolding her children for leaving the refrigerator door open and letting the milk spoil. Her eyes darted around the room, searching the face of each woman and daring any one of them to admit it.

"Look," she said, moving toward the doorway again, "I don't know WHAT kind of scheme y'all are mixed up in. I don't even WANT to know! But I can tell you one thing! I'm not here for it! Y'all got the wrong one this time!" She yanked at the purse strap that kept slipping off of her shoulder as she struggled to get her shoes on, emphasizing her decision to leave.

She took a step back into the room, looked around again. "I know y'all don't have money like that! You—" she pointed at Tanisha, "I just saw you in the parking lot begging the repo man not to take your car the other day! And you—" she stabbed a finger at Adriane, "You just asked me to let you hold $35 for your light bill this morning!"

Ruth stood up, hand outstretched toward Julene, trying not to laugh. She needed to stop the rant before anyone else's personal business was exposed, and she wanted Julene to take her seriously.

"Come on back in here, girl. It's not what you think. I should have told you earlier, but I just figured that you'd understand everything once you were here. When your turn comes around, you'll get your money too."

Chapter Thirteen

After Julene's outburst, the women gathered into a tighter circle and explained the process to their newest members. The cause for her alarm was understandable. If someone were to take an informal survey of the group, they would uncover a generous mix of food stamps, past-due bills, less than half-full gas tanks, overdrawn bank accounts, IOUs, and second jobs. These weren't wealthy women, they were the polar opposite. Julene knew this to be true about her new friends, but her friends didn't know everything about her.

"I'm sorry I reacted like that, y'all." Julene's eyes gleamed with tears that were too stubborn to fall, and she continued to speak. "It's just that I've been through a lot. So much has happened to me, things that you just wouldn't believe. And I've tried to put that stuff in the past, but sometimes … I'm just real sensitive about certain subjects, and money is a big one. I'm struggling, y'all. I'm struggling to provide for my babies and I just don't want no trouble. I can't afford to be mixed up in anything that could hurt my babies or threaten my freedom, and whenever I see that much money in an envelope, it usually involves something illegal." She looked toward Ruth pleadingly, "Please tell me it's not illegal."

Ruth smiled at Julene, noting for the first time that something delicate and fragile was hidden beneath her streetwise demeanor. She looked toward Tamara who sat rooted to her seat, looking uncomfortable to say the least. "It is definitely not illegal, Julene. You can probably explain it best, Cynthia. Go 'head and break it down for them," Ruth nodded toward Cynthia.

"So ... we basically started a rotating savings club a few years ago. Every pay period, each one of us puts a certain amount of money into the pot, so to speak. I hold the money. Each person also picks a month, and that's when they will receive their hand—their payout. So, most of us usually pick our birth month. But Monica," she winked at a woman who was deeply involved with a kabob at that moment, "Monica likes to get hers before Black Friday. And Elisha," she nodded at a woman who was collecting empty glasses and plates, "Elisha gets hers around Christmas to help with her shopping. Whatever you put in, that's what you get out. I'm the treasurer," she said, tapping her notebook. "I keep the ledger of deposits and payouts in here."

She rifled through the notebook and pulled out a slim receipt book. "I give everyone a receipt when I collect their money, and I keep a carbon copy of it for my records. So, for example, there were ten of us before you two joined, and we each put in $50 every other week when we get paid. That's $100 a month, per person. So, a month after we started, the first person received their hand—their $1,000 payout. And it just keeps rotating from there until everybody gets their money."

Cynthia flipped the notebook over and over in her hands. "Um, what else? Oh! It only works when everyone puts in like they promise, but we haven't had any problems with that in a long time. A few years back, we had to let a few members go because we always had to hunt them down just to get their contribution. But, for the most part, it's not hard to stick to it because you know that someone else is depending on you to put your money in. So that keeps us all honest."

Elisha walked in from the kitchen and joined the conversation. "It's not that you make any money from the club, it's just the same money that you put in, like Cynthia said. But it sure helps me to save a little bit of money through the year! I'm always broke around Christmas, especially if that direct deposit doesn't hit at the right time!" She laughed with a few other women in the circle. "So, my payout comes just in time for me to do my Christmas shopping."

Miss Emma Lee, the head cashier in the hospital cafeteria and also the oldest member of the club, began to speak and everyone quieted down so that her soft voice could be heard. "This isn't a new thing, the group savings. It's actually based on a Caribbean—or is it African?—tradition that women used for saving money. It's called a sou-sou. It has been passed down through the generations in our culture, even though most young people have gotten away from it. But ask your grandma. She probably knows about it. My mother and the women in the community where I grew up used to do it too. Now, women didn't work back then, unless they were cleaning houses or keeping kids for the white folks, so they didn't have much money. On top of that, either they didn't have access to the banks or they didn't trust the banks, so they needed another option for saving up their money.

"They would pinch off a little money from their husbands or save a little bit of the change that they earned themselves, but they would put it in the pot with the other women's money and wait for their payout to come around. And you know, I used to ask my mama why she didn't just save her own money, put it under the mattress like my daddy did. She had two reasons: one, she didn't want him to know that she had money." She smiled as she remembered her mother's lesson. "Gotta have your own money. She called it "mad money" because she would always use it to go shopping whenever she was mad at him. And two, she felt like she would spend it if she could get to it easily, so it was best for somebody else to hold it."

Everyone was nodding, acknowledging their own lack of financial discipline, unified in their struggles. Irene spoke up. "I know that even if I did save up $1,000 in my bank account, either the government would get it, or I would be like 'Oh, extra money? Let me buy these shoes!' Retail therapy, right? I always get in trouble when it comes to money." She looked around the room, taking in Cynthia's decor. "I see that I'm not alone. Somebody in here really loves some Target!" She winked at Cynthia and Cynthia laughed out loud. "Guilty. I'm guilty as charged, but I'm not the only one! If I go down, everybody goes down." She slowly pointed one gel-nailed finger around the room like a lightsaber, convicting each one of her friends until they were all laughing.

"Alright, alright! Back to business." Cynthia was in front of the group again. "So, Julene? Tamara? Are you in?"

Chapter Fourteen

"M iss Ruth?" Julene's soft tapping on the door sounded like she wasn't sure if she wanted to come in or not. She didn't want to wake Ruth's sleeping patient.

Ruth closed her Bible, stood up, and stretched. She felt like she'd been sitting in that corner for two days. She looked at her watch. 4:35 a.m. "What's up, Julene?"

Julene, not usually one to struggle for words, didn't know what to say. "Well, um, what time is your break? I just wanted to talk to you about something." Ruth was immediately concerned for her friend, her face asking all her questions at once. Julene smiled quickly and said, "Everything is fine. I'm okay. I just wanted to run something by you, get your opinion. Plus, I brought you some World Famous, Better-Than-Starbucks, Hospital Cafeteria coffee!" She held up two small Styrofoam cups and handed one to Ruth.

Ruth looked into the cup. "I just love the way that the powdered non-dairy creamer clumps up on top of my coffee!" Her nose hovered over the rim of the cup and she inhaled deeply. "Thanks, Ju. Okay, so what's up?"

Julene blurted out the question that had been bothering her since the book club meeting. "This savings club—the sou-sou. Does it really work?"

A slow smile blossomed across Ruth's face and she sighed in relief. "Girl, you had me worried! Yeah, the club works." "But, in this day and age, why are you still doing it? I mean, I get it about the retail therapy and everything, but it just seems like it could be doing more for you. For everybody to be struggling all of the time, that's a lot of money that y'all are handling!"

Ruth thought about it. Thought about each of her friends and their situations. They all struggled. Despite their hard work and second jobs, they just struggled. They had poor credit, minimal financial literacy, low-paying jobs, children and grandchildren, abusive husbands, no husbands, medical problems. The list was endless and, year after year, things just didn't change much in the community. Unless someone hit the number or it was tax season, there was little "extra" money. And, ironically, when everybody is broke including you, the broke life starts to feel uncomfortably normal.

There was a hint of defeat in her voice when she answered Julene. "It's been the best way for me to save money, especially in the days when I had to hide money from my husband. Plus, it's kind of fun having a goal and saving with friends and challenging each other. It's sort of like doing a diet or working out, it's more fun and you'll have a better chance of sticking with it if someone does it with you. Do you know we started out contributing $10 each? Now we're up to $100 a month!"

Julene understood that line of reasoning. She didn't have any savings herself. She'd always struggled to keep money and she'd been known to break down and splurge on expensive sneakers for her kids or dinners at the Olive Garden with her boyfriend. She had always thought that, with a better job and more money, she'd be able to get ahead, but she sometimes feared that it would never happen. There was always something the kids needed, something wrong with the car, the dog, her cousin, the neighbor, her student loans—money seemed to elude her without mercy.

"You know, when I was working for that attorney, we represented some very wealthy clients. I mean, RICH people. And one thing that I saw them do to build their wealth and keep their money was to set up a trust. Basically, they would put their family money together in a trust and use it for investments, college tuitions, mortgages, and stuff. So, instead of going to get a loan from the bank and paying the bank interest on that borrowed money for years, they used the money from the trust and paid it back to themselves with interest. That's how they were able to grow the family money and afford the things that they wanted without going through banks and lenders. And that's how those families were able to keep their money instead of throwing it all away.

"One of the attorneys explained it to me like this: Say someone took out a bank loan for a mortgage and the monthly payment was like $1,500 for thirty years. First of all, ain't nobody got $1,500 a month unless they're a doctor or something!" Julene laughed out loud, forgetting for a moment that it was almost five in the morning and Ruth had a sleeping patient. "Anyway, every month, the bank is going to take their interest out when you make that payment. That's how they pay themselves for giving you the loan. So, you're paying—or somebody is paying—$1,500 a month for their house, the bank is taking $800 of it for interest, some of the money goes for taxes or whatever, and they're only applying, like $400 toward the balance of the loan. THAT'S why it takes thirty years to pay off a doggone house!! Because most of your payment is going to the interest instead of the balance of the loan. And that's ONLY IF your credit is good enough to get the loan in the first place!

"Imagine if your family was the 'bank?' And by family, I mean our club. Imagine if that $800 a month was building up in our trust rather than the pockets of the CEO over at the bank?"

If Julene had been holding a microphone, she would have dropped it right then. She was pleased with herself at having made her point so clearly. She had worried about how to start the conversation, how to explain it all, but once she began to speak, the words just seemed to flow.

Ruth looked at her, smiling as though her friend had just told her that cows *do*, in fact, jump over the moon. "Girl, what in the world does that have to do with me? I don't have a house, good credit, or $1,500 a month! I took the down payment for my trailer out of my retirement, and there's nothing about me that says 'bank.' I try not to borrow money from anybody, and I try not to lend it either."

Julene was stunned. How could Ruth not get it? "OKAY, Miss Ruth. First of all, do you know how much the IRS is going to penalize you for taking that money out of your retirement? You ain't gonna get nothing back when tax season comes! But, that's a whole other subject. Now, what if, instead of saving money for Black

Friday junk or Christmas presents, we pooled that money together and formed our own trust? What if we changed our attitudes about money? What if we decided to quit being broke? We can help each other to stay on track. It's easier—you said it yourself! And what if we start building our own wealth? Something's got to change, and why can't it be us? Look, y'all have already laid the foundation, why not put it toward something that matters? That's what a trust is. It's not just money for today. It's wealth that you build for future generations."

Ruth side-eyed the little bundle of energy that Julene had become. She hated talking about money and there was so much that she had never learned about it. How do you learn about something you don't have? Something that your mama never had, and your grandma either?

"Okay, look, Miss Ruth. Can I suggest the next book club book?"

Ruth raised an eyebrow, intrigued.

Julene pushed forward and made her proposal. "I would like to read this book that I heard about at the law firm where I used to work in Chicago. I mean, we *do* read books in this club, right? Not just use it as an excuse to pass out money? Maybe if we educate ourselves, we would be able to come together to make something major happen. I watched how they did things when I was at the law firm, and I remember that the attorneys always gave their clients a few books to read as part of their financial management consultations."

Ruth shook her head, "They won't go for it. I can tell you that right now. We've never read anything like that."

Julene was not deterred. "Come on Miss Ruth, open your mind. The Lord don't have it for us to be in bondage for the rest of our lives, and poverty is bondage. And debt is a sin! 'Plant a seed in good soil and ye shall grow a good crop.' 'Lead not to your own understanding!'" She grinned. "I know my Word."

"Bless your heart. You're a mess! A 'Get Rich Quick' book? I'll talk to the rest about it, but don't count on it. All they like to read are murder mysteries and biographies." Ruth was laughing as she ushered Julene away from the door. "Let me get back in there with my patient."

Before she closed the door, she stuck her head out, "And it's 'lean' not on your own understanding, not 'lead!'"

Back inside the room, sunlight was creeping around the edges of the window curtains, casting a warm glow on her patient's cheek. The sun was on duty. The moon had been dismissed.

Chapter Fifteen

One would assume that, after an eight-hour shift in sterilization and an overnight one-to-one, a person would be practically incapacitated from sleep deprivation. Exhausted. That assumption failed royally when it came to Ruth. After the conversation with Julene, Ruth took advantage of the bright and crispy-aired morning and slipped out of her sleeping patient's room to head toward the riverfront greenway for a four-mile walk.

On the backside of the town's most exclusive neighborhood, the greenway snaked beneath the trees, at times following the curvature of the river and at times drifting back toward the massive homes that surrounded the community's golf course. The greenway was unusually quiet this morning and she noticed that, when the pathway neared the water's edge, she could actually hear the lapping sound of the water coming together with the muddy bank and exposed tree roots. It had a rank, fungal smell, and she loved it.

Each time she inhaled, she instinctively wrinkled her nose at the stench, but she continued to inhale deeply. She practiced the cleansing breaths her aerobics instructor often encouraged.

There were snakes in the water, and, on some of her walks, she had yielded to a few of the thick black reptiles that occasionally found themselves caught in the center of the walkway. She would wait patiently for them to wriggle toward the underbrush as though someone had inconsiderately thrown a sidewalk through their habitat in the middle of the night. Her skin crawled at the thought of the free-spirited folks who went tubing in that murky water whenever the weather was warm.

Following the pathway as it curved away from the water, the backsides of the mammoth homes presented a different landscape. Most were designed with second or third-floor decks and patios. She could tell which homeowners preferred to enjoy the river front view without the company of flies and mosquitoes. Those were the homes with huge windows and Florida rooms instead of open patios. Ruth could relate to that. If she lived here, she would be content to just look out at the view rather than actually be a part of the view.

She knew that some of the doctors lived out here. She also knew of a few people from her side of town who worked out here. Julene's words niggled at the back of her mind. The wealthy people that she spoke of lived out here. *The RICH people.* Ruth could be honest with herself and say that she didn't desire to live among these people or own a home this huge. She didn't need all that space, and who was going to clean it, anyway? Struggle had always been a theme in her life, but she didn't covet money or things. True, things would be easier if her money situation loosened up a little bit. If she could give up the sitter shift, visit her daughter more, quit going to the payday loan place. Times had always been tough, but they could always be tougher too.

The thing that she couldn't deny was the way that people of other cultures took care of each other and protected their finances, the way they lived more frugally and kept their money circulating within their own communities. The Latinos, the Jews, the Indians, the Asians, the Greeks. And now, according to Julene, the white folks had a system for raising and training their families to build and manage wealth too. Everyone was taking care of their own. Everyone except for the blacks.

Julene hadn't necessarily revealed any new or hidden information to Ruth. You could just look around the community and spot the people who had old money. Family money. The ones who had businesses and community centers named after their grandfathers. She'd always known that the wealth wasn't spread evenly in the community, but until now, she just hadn't given any thought as to the reasons why or how some families kept it going for so many generations. She hadn't been raised to be financially savvy in the traditional sense. She had been raised to survive.

Don't you e-ver stop learning! Granddaddy Fields' voice seemed so clear that she was inclined to glance backward, as though he might be standing nearby. He was no longer around, but he had driven the message into her mind when she was a child and she never forgot his lessons. His rules. *Don't stop learning. Don't stop reading. Ain't no way you can learn if you don't read.*

With no formal education beyond grade school, he was easily the most intelligent man she had ever known. His was the face she pictured during her black history studies in grade school. To her, he *was* black history. In her mind, he was an abolitionist, an innovator, an educator. He consumed books like they were food. He always started with the Bible, but he didn't stop there, and he didn't limit himself to any specific genre. History, fiction, slave narratives, mythology, cookbooks, old textbooks, classic literature—the constant reading was the reason that he moved out of his wife's bedroom into the back room when they were still a young couple. Ruth's grandmother had complained that his late-night reading and nightlight were disturbing her beauty rest.

By virtue of his training, Ruth felt obliged to at least consider the book that Julene had suggested and the idea that she was proposing. She understood her young friend's frustration and optimism. Julene's intelligence far exceeded the mediocre life that she led, and that made her no different than most of the women in the community. But Ruth, being more mature, was tired of chasing dreams. Over the years, she and each of her friends had tried their hands at all sorts of entrepreneurial endeavors. They had sold makeup, vacuum cleaners, shoes, and cakes. They took online certificate courses in early childhood development, event planning, and medical assisting. They sold dinners from their homes and attempted to start a community garden. Irene had once run an illegal bingo hall out of the shed behind her trailer.

Ruth had worked doggishly to propel her daughter out into the world, to give her the opportunity to enjoy a better life than her own. She decided that her daughter's successes would be her reward. Her daughter hadn't necessarily soared to the heights that Ruth had envisioned. She hadn't quite found her way yet.

These days, the most that Ruth could hope for was to get lucky at bingo night or hit the number with the lottery ticket that she chipped in for with the third-floor nurses every Thursday. The problem was, she knew darn well that things could have been better. *Should* have been better.

Her ancestors had planted some seeds in their lifetimes for which they knew they wouldn't live to see the fruits. In their era, they had laid the foundations for personal freedom, civil rights, equal opportunities, peace. They took wild, calculated risks on ideologies that were unheard of for people in their time.

For the future generations, they fought for a quality of life that should have been enjoyed by all but was, back then, only being enjoyed by a select few. Many of their efforts and endeavors had come to pass in extraordinary ways, not for the frontline soldiers, but for their children and grandchildren.

She thought about the seeds that her generation had sown for the next generations. Not much, compared to the incredible strides that their ancestors had made, many of them literally paying the cost with their lives. What would she leave for her granddaughter's future children— socially or economically? After purchasing her trailer, there was nothing left to leave them or anyone else. No inheritance to be divided.

If *anybody* has done it, then anybody *CAN* do it. These words, in Granddaddy Fields' voice, rang in her ears.

Back in her car, Ruth pulled out her phone and dialed her granddaughter's number.

"Hey, Grandma! I miss you!" Toot's smiling face appeared on the phone screen.

"Hey baby, I miss you too! What you been up to?" Ruth held the phone at arm's length to get a better view of her only grandchild.

"Nothing. Mommy finally let me get some apps on my phone and I got Instagram too! Did you see the picture I tagged you in? It was the one from when you came to visit us last summer!"

"No, I didn't see it. I think I need you to come out and help me again. I can't remember my password."

Toot was laughing, smiling into the phone, her braces decorated with neon pink elastics.

"You still got those braces on, I see. I thought you were supposed to have them off by now?" Ruth tilted her phone to the left, struggling to eliminate the glare.

"I know, ugh!" Toot's eye-rolling was worthy of an Oscar. "My other grandma said she would pay for it, but then she went to the casino cruise in Biloxi and when she got back, she said she couldn't do it. And then, Mommy was supposed to take me to get them off but then she said we had to wait until she gets her income tax back. She said she didn't have the money to get them off right now. So, I called my daddy and he said she needed to take the money out of the child supp—Grandma, what? I see you shaking your head! Did I say something wrong?"

Ruth looked at the phone, realized that her granddaughter could see her expression, and forced a smile. "Nothing, nothing baby. I know you can't wait to get them off, so I know you're excited!"

"Grandma! Tell me. I'm almost thirteen, you know! I know there's something else. But I know what you're going to say, 'it's grown folks' business', right? Y'all never tell me *anything*!"

Ruth laughed. "Can't get nothing by you. And yes, it is grown folk's business. Tell your mama to call me later." She kissed the screen on the phone. Toot's kissing sounds were muffled as they came through the speaker just as the battery in Ruth's phone died.

CHAPTER SIXTEEN

T hanks for giving me a ride. I'll give you some gas money when we get paid." Irene was sitting in the passenger's seat of Ruth's car, mindlessly flipping through the book that had been lying on the floorboard. "Huh-nee! My kids, I swear! I thought that I would have been finished raising them once they'd graduated from high school, but no ... seems like I'm still raising them even though they have children of their *own*!" She stopped flipping through the book. "And here I go, letting my son use my car, feeling sorry for him because the Auto Money place has his, and he has to pick his kids up from school all this week. Now, he told me that he was getting paid yesterday and he was supposed to pick his car up. Come to find out, he hadn't even worked enough hours to cover the amount that he owes on the car, so he *still* couldn't get it out! And that's with his whole paycheck! This boy, Lord Je-sus! Help me, Father! This boy don't make enough money to pay for the car that he needs to use to get to work to pay for the car! How is it that you are so broke that you can't even afford to get to work? So now, he's using *my* car and *I'm* the one catching a ride!" She went back to flipping through the book.

Ruth looked at her sideways. "So, what are you going to do? You can't afford for something to happen to your car. You remember the last time, when it started running hot while he was driving it and then he just parked it in your yard and didn't even tell you?"

Irene blew off a heavy breath and stopped flipping the pages. "I know. I'm thinking what I might do is give him the rest of the money so he can get his car out and give me my car back."

Ruth raised an eyebrow but kept her eyes on the road.

"I know! I know!" Irene slapped her own leg with the book and looked at the side of Ruth's face. "I keep bailing him out! He has my grandbabies, though! And I've already paid for Alyssa's cheer camp, and they don't give refunds, so if he can't get her there every day, then I'm out of that money too. I have a few dollars left over from my birth month payout. I was planning to use it for the chiropractor, but I guess I need to get everyone else situated first."

Irene picked the book up again, turning it over and over in her hands, looking at the cover, her mind a million miles away. "I'm telling you the truth. Whose book is this?" She held the book up toward Ruth.

Ruth glanced over at the book, shrugged a shoulder. "That's the book that Julene wants us to read for book club.

Remember the one I told you about the other day?"

Irene looked the book over closely. "Yeah, I remember. I

didn't know you already had it though."

"Well, I figured nobody else would want to read it," her explanation was laced with inexplicable guilt. "But I kind of wanted to check it out, just to see, and it was sitting on the shelf in the used bookstore, so I picked it up."

"Does it have something to do with making money?" Irene was half-joking, half-serious. "Honey, I wish I had done better and made some better choices with mine! You know, that's one of the reasons me and Dennis ended up divorced. Don't get me wrong, he got on my d—he got on my last nerve! But he was good with money. I used to think he was so stingy! I mean, he wouldn't spend money on a piece of toilet paper if the thought he could steal a roll from his job!"

Irene was laughing, remembering how they'd butted heads whenever money was spent. "He just couldn't stand it when I would help my kids out, and he didn't have any kids, so he just didn't get it. And maybe he was right. He was definitely smart about money, wasn't never broke. But I couldn't have no man telling me what I can't do for my own children. They're always going to be my kids. If they need me, I'm here." She sighed. "He used to say that I was enabling them instead of helping them. He was probably right about that part."

Ruth's car had come to a stop in front of Irene's trailer. Gathering her lunch bag and purse, Irene stopped and looked at her old friend. "So, this book's going to teach me how to think about growing rich, huh?"

Ruth shrugged a shoulder, her smile ambiguous.

Tossing the book onto the seat, Irene stood outside of the car. "Well, shoot, let's read it and see! What do we have to lose?"

CHAPTER SEVENTEEN

"Courage is not the absence of fear, but rather the assessment that something else is more important than fear."

—Franklin D. Roosevelt

The energy in Cynthia's dining room was palpable, and the festive atmosphere was the perfect backdrop for the evening. Cynthia had draped the dining table with a black and red cloth, and then sprinkled it with gold confetti. She managed to find an assortment of gold and white serving dishes at the thrift store, and the party food was on full display.

For the menu, she had chosen teriyaki chicken wings, egg rolls, tortilla chips with black-eyed pea salsa, a veggie and cheese platter, meatballs, chocolate-covered strawberries, bacon-wrapped brussels sprouts, and seafood salad. Champagne flutes and sparkling wine were arranged on a gold serving tray at the end of the table. In the center of the table, a large glass vase was filled with colorful note cards that were folded in half.

"Cynthia, you outdo yourself every time!" Irene stood at the head of the table holding her macaroni. "Where am I supposed to put this?"

"Right here! I saved a spot just for you!" Cynthia pointed toward the space between the chicken wings and the egg rolls.

After everyone had eaten and mingled with one another, Cynthia tapped the side of her glass with a fork and addressed her friends. "So, ladies, how about that book? I don't know about you all, but I think it definitely changed something in me! I kind of feel like I want to change my attitude about what I want in my life. Like I want to make a fresh start. And I know I'm not the only one!"

She looked around the room and saw that she had everyone's full attention.

"So, in the spirit of new beginnings," she fanned her hand around the festively decorated dining room, "tonight's theme is New Year's Eve. To mark the eve of a fresh start for all of us!"

Looking at the faces of her friends, she challenged, "Don't tell me that I'm the only one who feels like she can do better. Correction: has to do better!"

Understanding and agreeability spread across the faces of the ladies in the room and smiles began to emerge.

Julene was the first to jump onboard. "You're right. She's right, y'all. This book is like an instruction manual that tells you how to stop making excuses and take responsibility for your financial life."

Cynthia was encouraged by Julene's enthusiasm. "Okay, then! Y'all had me worried for a minute! How could you not get fired up by a book like this? Alright, for our celebration, I came up with a little activity. Please take a note card from the vase in the center of the table and let's meet in the den. Don't open it! Just take one and meet me in there."

In the den, there was murmuring and whispering as the ladies tried to guess what Cynthia had in mind. "I'm not playing Truth or Dare! Y'all don't even want to know what kind of skeletons I have hidden in my closet!" Ruth pretended to bite her nails and cover her face in embarrassment.

Cynthia took the floor. "So first, let's thank Julene for suggesting such an awesome book!" There was a round of applause. "I can say that I enjoyed reading something that changed my attitude about the way that I choose to live my life. And I know that we all want to do better financially, so it was a real eye-opener."

Julene stood up. "I'm just sick of trying to go exempt on my paycheck just to get a few more dollars in my hand every month!"

Elisha gave her a high-five. "I know that's right! Especially in those months when we get paid three times!" The room erupted with laughter, each lady intimately experienced in the art of working the system to stretch her paycheck a little more.

"Okay, okay, and since I think we can all agree that there were a lot of important lessons in each chapter," Cynthia held a note card in the air, "I've printed one on each of these cards."

Ruth smiled, "What do we have to do, act each one out? Is this some kind of charades game?"

Cynthia pretended to think it over. "Hmm, it's not too late to change the rules a little ... Okay Ruth, since you spoke up first, why don't you read yours? After you read it, use one of these thumbtacks to pin it to this board." She held up a poster-sized vision board and a small container filled with gold-colored push pins.

Ruth looked at her card. "Irene, I need your glasses." Staring at her card again, she smiled, "Mine says *'Transform your sexual desire into fuel to achieve your goal.'*"

"Alright, girl!" Tamara was laughing and winking at Ruth.

Around the room, the ladies read off their cards:

"Have absolute faith, no matter what."

"Use positive self-talk as you repeat your goal to yourself twice daily."

"Form a mastermind group to share, motivate, and solve problems."

"Be persistent. Never ever give up."

"Specialize. Become an expert in one area of focus." "Be in love with your goal with a burning desire."

"What the mind can believe, the mind can achieve."

"Form a plan and take massive action to achieve your goal."

"Listen to your gut."

"Reprogram your beliefs with positivity and confidence."

"Be open to God's will."

When they were finished, Cynthia held up the completed vision board: "This is awesome, ladies! Just imagine us all coming together to get our affairs in order! Imagine having the resources to purchase real estate, send our children to college, pay for weddings, or start businesses without having to sit in front of some bank lender and beg for help!"

Tamara held up her hand. "I liked the book and everything, but some of it had me feeling confused. I don't want to sound dumb, but what was the secret? The book kept talking about unlocking this 'secret' and revealing the 'secret,' but I must have missed it. I feel like, if you know what you want to do with your life, but need some motivation, then this book would be great. I'm going to have my son read it. He's been trying to get his fashion design career going. He started a YouTube channel and everything, but he just keeps getting discouraged and distracted. It would be a great book for him. But there wasn't some deep secret hidden in there that really applied to me, per se."

Julene scooted toward the edge of her seat. "That's kind of what I was hoping we'd get to talk about." She glanced at Ruth and continued, somewhat nervously, "Maybe the point isn't for the book to give you the secret, exactly, but I bet it stepped on your toes a few times. And which one of us doesn't want to take control of our lives instead of just accepting whatever comes our way?

"I think this book sort of prepares your mind to work harder for what you want. To be more passionate about whatever God has placed in your heart and to set your own intentions for what you want to accomplish in this life." She paused, swallowed, and spoke with more confidence. "So, if you know what you want, this book teaches you how to use your faith and persistence to get it. And it explains how to avoid the obstacles that trip people up sometimes."

Ruth added on to Julene's interpretation. "The author was basically saying that if you get focused, then you can use the power of the mind to change your situation. And, honestly, some of it sounded a little hippy-ish at first, but it sort of lines up with the teachings of the Bible. You know, prayer, meditation, and commitment to a vision."

"What I want is to be in a better financial situation. I don't want to end up like my mama, unable to afford independent living, depending on Lord knows who to take care of me." Cynthia motioned toward her mother's room down the hall.

"I have custody of my grandchildren now." Ms. Emma Lee sat up straighter in her chair. "I wish I had more to give them. I want to get my affairs situated so that they'll be okay if anything happens to me."

Ruth and Irene looked at each other, concern registering on both their faces. Irene spoke first. "So, you have full custody of them now?"

Ms. Emma Lee exhaled a burdened breath. "Yeah, I got them full-time now. Their parents ain't a bit of good, not that mother of theirs nor my son. I'm the only stability in their lives, so I have to do right by them. I can't sit and watch them be neglected. But I'm old. I'm seventy-three this year. Too old to be raising a fourth grader and a fifth grader. I was hoping to be retired by now, but as long as I have my babies, I guess I'll be ringing up soups and salads until the Lord calls me home."

Ruth nodded her head, understanding a grandmother's plight, but sorry to see Ms. Emma Lee starting all over when she should have already been retired. She was still a beautiful woman, her velvety brown skin only hinted at her true age, but the weariness in her eyes recounted every year that she'd lived. She was tired. "A fourth- and a fifth-grader? That's a handful! Are they the two you always bring to vacation Bible school in the summertime? What were their names?"

"Mecca and Amethyst. Yeah, those are my babies." Ms. Emma Lee laughed out loud when she spoke their names. "I tried to get their mama to give them some cup names, but she had her mind set on picking out names that she thought were unique." She paused, noticing the quizzical expressions on everyone's faces. "Cup names. You know, like names that the kids could find on a cup when they go to Disney World! Everywhere you go, they sell these personalized things for kids—cups, books, license plates for bicycles—my babies will never find anything with their names on them!"

She waited for everyone to get it, and then they were all laughing. When she caught her breath, Ms. Emma Lee spoke again. "What I really want is for somebody to help me set up some kind of savings for my babies. Something that their parents can't touch. Something that will be there for them when I'm not around anymore. I remember when we first agreed to read this book, Julene had mentioned that her old boss was the one to set up the trusts for her clients. Maybe it's time for us to do that. I'm old. It's too late for me, but y'all are younger, I know you want to retire some day and I know I have to at least make some arrangements for my grandbabies."

The women in the room were nodding slowly, realizing that they might have just stumbled upon their mission. They all needed to get together with Julene's old boss, not just Ms. Emma Lee. And she was right to want to prevent her adult children from accessing the funds. It wasn't fair to make the grandchildren suffer because of their parent's choices.

"You know what, Ms. Emma? You're right. I need to get something situated for my grandbabies, too, and my kids don't need to know nothing about it! I'm telling you, it's like they can smell money on me, and they just come a-running! Come out of the woodworks!" Irene's expression was suddenly earnest, and her voice was somber. "Whatever it is, I don't want anyone to know about it. Let's just do what we have to do, get it all together—make it legal, you know?—and just go on about our business like nothing has changed."

Julene spoke again. "I'll reach out to my old boss and ask for some advice. In the meantime, I suggest that we build up a little savings. Maybe we can keep putting the money in, but stop doing the payouts, because I know that you have to have some money to start a fund, but I don't know how much."

Tamara cleared her throat. "I like the sound of this, so don't get me wrong, but I don't have money to just sit to the side like that and not able to use it. I can put in a few dollars for right now, but are we still talking about $100 a month? Because I need to send some money to my son. He has fashion week coming up. I can put a few dollars in the pot, but not all of it right now."

"Nope. Not happening." Irene's voice was dead-serious. "Either you're in or you're out. We're trying to do something different here and we got to help each other stick to it. First thing we have to do is leave our grown children out of it! He'll thank you later. Now, like the book said, you've gotta decide if you want the money to flow toward you or away from you." She leaned forward for emphasis. "And if you're going to stop the money from flowing toward me, then I can't roll with you." She paused, composed herself, and drew a heart shape in the air with her fingers. "This is all said in love, now. It's all love, honey."

Cynthia held a hand up. "Ladies, I think Irene is right. It's just like the sou-sou, it won't work unless we're all in and we hold one another accountable. So, Tamara, are you in?"

Tamara looked at Irene and winked an eye. "You make me so sick sometimes!"

Irene blew her a kiss. "Have the children, don't let them have you!"

Cynthia breathed a sigh of relief. "Alright. Can we touch and agree on this right now?"

"Wait a minute!" Julene stood up abruptly. "I did work with the attorney who handled these things, but I was mainly like her secretary and her personal assistant. I don't know the exact details about how she did it, but I know that her clients loved her, so she must have been helping them to make some money.

"All of you are saying that we need to move forward and take the next step, but honestly, it makes me a little nervous. I mean, back when I first suggested the savings and investment thing, I knew it was the right thing to do, but, it's like, I can't believe that it's really happening! If things don't work out, I just don't want everyone looking at me like it's my fault."

Cynthia held the vision board up and began reading the words aloud. "Faith, believe, achieve, positive, confidence, persistence ..." She placed the board on the table and stood up. "The book said that you need the support of a mastermind group, right? Isn't that us?"

A sheepish expression flickered across Julene's face, followed by a demure half-smile, "I'll reach out to her, find out what she recommends and let everyone know. Does that sound like a plan?"

Ms. Emma Lee's eyes twinkled. "That sounds good, baby. But don't take too long. I'm an old lady, might not have much time left!"

Ruth swatted her hand in Ms. Emma Lee's direction, "You stop that, now! You're not old, you're just seasoned! You'll probably outlive all of us!"

The ladies stood and joined hands. Heads were bowed, and Cynthia's soft voice filled the room. *"Lord, we come to thank you tonight. We're so glad that you saw fit to bless us with the love and friendship that we share. Thank you for bringing us together. I believe that we can do something that we've never done before, and God I'm just asking you to guide us, Lord. Show us the way that you would have us to go. Because Lord, we want to do what is pleasing in your sight. We want to operate in decency and in order, in accordance with your will. So, Lord, speak to us. Speak through us. Help us to blaze a new path, Lord. Not for ourselves, but for our families, for our communities. We love you, God, and we glorify your name. And for your precious son, we say amen."*

CHAPTER EIGHTEEN

The next time that the book club met, the theme was all business. There were no signature drinks, no fancy hors d'oeuvres. There was only a room filled with women who were unwavering in their determination to take a massive step toward their futures. The meeting was held in the hospital's executive board room.

"So, *this* is where the big-wigs come to get away from us." Ruth's eyes scanned the colossal boardroom table, the brushed nickel fixtures, the interactive whiteboard.

"Yeah, just look at this view. How could you get any work done with this beautiful view?" Irene, dwarfed by the floor-to-ceiling windows, was hypnotized by the landscape.

When the ladies had all filed into the room, Cynthia locked the door behind them and called the meeting to order. "So, I'm glad that everyone could be here for this quick meeting. I felt that it was best for us to touch base as soon as possible rather than waiting until our regular monthly meeting if we want to keep ourselves motivated. Now, I know it's been a long day and everyone is ready to get home, so let's get down to business. Julene?"

Julene moved to the front of the room and took a minute to acknowledge each woman at the table with a smile. "Look at us! No, look at God! One day, this will be *our* boardroom!" The women looked around at themselves, bumping elbows and settling into the huge leather chairs, testing the feeling of entitlement.

Julene spoke more seriously. "Alright, well my assignment was to reach out to my old boss lady and find out what she recommends for our next step. I told her that we had saved—how much have we saved?" She glanced over at Cynthia.

Cynthia flipped through her tattered notebook. "Um, about $6,000."

Julene grinned. "Okay, well I told her that we had a little more than that, but anyways, she was pretty impressed with us. So—" she paused and looked around the room. "Good job!"

Moving toward the whiteboard, Julene continued speaking. "She said that we need to establish some rules, elect some leaders, and do some more reading. She said that we need," she fished a folded piece of paper out of her pocket and unfolded it, "a treasurer. I guess that would be you, Cynthia. Do we need to set up a bank account for the money? I never asked where you keep it."

All eyes were on Cynthia, who swallowed with some difficulty, caught off-guard. "The money? It's in the safe. I always keep it in the petty cash safe downstairs. I used to keep it in a bank account that Mama doesn't use anymore, but I had to move it because the government was trying to count it as part of her assets, which was messing with her social security. I figured that the petty cash safe would be the most secure location without having to be reported through the banks."

"That might be okay for now, but it's time for us to start thinking of a better, long-term solution." Julene continued, "Okay, we need a presiding partner—that's kind of like the president or the person who runs the meetings—and we need a secretary to keep the minutes and make sure that everyone is informed.

"I don't mind taking the role of secretary since I have some previous experience, and plus, I can keep the lines of communication open between us and my old boss lady. Her name is Tina, by the way. I guess we just need to vote and agree on a presiding officer, then."

She looked around the room, eyes asking for a nominee. Ruth poked Irene in the side and Irene laugh-coughed in response. Ruth stood up. "I nominate Irene. She's bossy enough and loud enough to run our meetings." The ladies were laughing, and before Irene could object, they had all said 'Aye.'

"Okay, then! It's settled." Julene wrote the names of the presiding partner, treasurer, and secretary on the whiteboard. Then, she referred back to her note. "She gave me two more books for us to read. She told me that this first one was written back in the 1920s, and it's a selection of short stories set during the ancient Babylon times, that teaches some basic principles about money management and budgeting. The second book—well maybe—" she looked up at the group. "Why don't we read this one for now and we can start the other one after our next meeting. Tina said we should definitely continue having regular business meetings for planning and organizational issues in additional to our actual reading discussions. What do you all think?"

Irene stood up, mostly business with a hint of mischief. "Everyone in favor of the next book selection and having regular meetings, say 'aye.' All who are opposed, say 'Nay.'"

The ladies said 'aye', and Irene banged an imaginary gavel on the table. "The aye's have it. This meeting is adjourned!"

After the meeting, Ruth walked over to the YMCA for a yoga class and a few miles on the treadmill. When she finished and was heading toward her car, she noticed that Julene was sitting on the bench near the hospital's side entrance. She pulled her car close to the curb and rolled the window down.

"You okay, Ju?"

Julene's annoyance was uncontained. "Yeah. No. Not really. I've been waiting for my ride since our meeting ended. He was supposed to be here two hours ago! Can I catch a ride with you? I stay in the Chantilly Apartments over there on Four Seasons Drive."

"Of course! I know exactly where that is." Ruth unlocked the doors and Julene flopped into the seat.

"I appreciate this. I don't have any cash on me, but I'll pay you for your gas when I see you tomorrow." Julene rested her head on the back of the seat and closed her eyes. "I'm so tired of this man! He's not the same man that he was when we moved here! I mean, he never would have left me sitting out there like that! He didn't even call to tell me that he wasn't coming. I'm just calling and calling him, getting sent straight to his voicemail. After an hour, he calls from some weird number and says that the car broke down and he was borrowing somebody's car to come get me. After another hour, I called the house and my baby girl answered the phone, telling me that they're home alone and scared."

Ruth looked over at Julene. "What in the world could he be up to? Do you think he's cheating on you?"

"That did cross my mind, but it seems like he just hangs around with this random bunch of guys from down there in Regal Manor all the time. I was actually starting to think that he might be gay. Especially when—" Her cellphone rang. She looked at Ruth, rolled her eyes and answered it. After listening for a moment, she simply hung up. She leaned back against the seat and closed her eyes again.

Ruth drove in silence, giving Julene time to compose herself.

"Can you believe it? Can you believe that he's trying to tell me that his phone died, and he couldn't get a ride to come get me? I can't!" She rolled her head toward the window and stared into the trees. "When I talked to my baby girl today, do you know she told me that she didn't get the perfect attendance award at school because he hasn't been taking her every day? She said sometimes Daddy doesn't wake her up on time, so he lets the kids stay home!"

When Ruth's car turned into the parking lot in front of Julene's apartment building, a homeless guy was pacing nervously in front of the staircase.

"There he is, right there!" Julene pointed in the direction of the homeless guy and Ruth's eyes scanned the parking lot, unsure of what she was looking at or who Julene was pointing toward.

"Do you mean the homeless person?" she asked hesitantly.

Julene choked back an irritated laugh. "He's not homeless, he just looks likes like a bum! I'm so sick of him, right now! This is what I'm talking about. I can do bad by myself." She got out of the car and slammed the door. In a second, she reappeared at Ruth's window. "Thank you, Miss Ruth, for the ride. I'm sorry for slamming your door."

"It's okay, Julene. You go deal with your man. I'll sit right here for a little bit to make sure you're okay."

As Julene walked toward the building, Ruth could hear the guy as he broke down into tears. Through tears, he was explaining that he had loaned her car to one of his friends and the guy had not brought the car back yet.

Julene was irate. Hollering in his face as though she would hit him. "You just let somebody borrow my car? Who was it?"

"I forgot his name! I mean, I know it, but I can't think of it right now."

"I'm calling the police." Julene pulled her phone out of her purse. "I'm reporting it stolen."

"No! Wait. Okay. I let him hold the car. I went over there to get high and I didn't have enough money, and he said I could get a hit if I let him hold the car. He said I wasn't getting it back until I had some money for him."

Julene sat on the bottom step and then immediately stood up again. "You sold my car? You gave my car away to a drug dealer! Are you a crackhead? What is it? Meth? Heroin? That's why all of my spoons are missing, isn't it? Oh my God! My spoons! You've been around my babies with that stuff?" Her voice was a shrill echo inside the building's breezeway. "Get away from me! Stay away from us!"

She disappeared up the staircase, bounding over the steps two at a time, and the now-homeless guy stood, staring up at the apartment building for a long second before turning around. For a moment, he seemed to be staring directly at Ruth, his face devoid of recognition, before he turned toward the street and walked away. His gait was swerving and unsteady, his posture broken, his silhouette becoming smaller and smaller, until he disappeared down the block.

Ruth sat in her car for several minutes, not sure what she had just seen, unsure of what she should do. Her phone rang. Julene's eerily calm voice came through clearly, "thanks for waiting, Miss Ruth. I can see your car from my window, but I'm okay. I called the police and told them the name of the apartment complex where he's been hanging out, so hopefully they can find my car. My neighbor said she would run me down to the police department if I need to go later.

Go and get some rest."

"I want you to call me if you need anything. Call me anyways and let me know that you're alright. Or if you need a ride to work. Or if the kids need something. Please." "I will. Promise." She hung up.

CHAPTER NINETEEN

After leaving Julene's apartment, Ruth headed home. She sat in the grassy parking space in front of her trailer, lowered the windows, and turned the car off. After a moment, she pulled her phone out of her cargo pocket and called her daughter.

When the call connected, a flurry of activity played across the screen. The ceiling of the car, a blur of trees past the car window, her daughter's forehead, and then her face come into view. "Hey, Mama!"

"Are you driving? You shouldn't be FaceTiming while you're driving!"

"You called me, Mama! It's not like I called you!" She was laughing. "Hold on."

More fumbling and then her face was centered squarely in the screen. "Okay. Now."

Ruth peered at the new, steady image on the screen. "What did you do? Sit the phone up on the dashboard? Is that how you've been driving around?"

"No ma'am. It's a phone mount that suction cups to the windshield. Hands-free! Safety first, right? Anyways, I texted you the other day. Toot said you wanted to talk to me."

"Right. Talk to you—not text. I need to see your face and hear your voice. That's why I don't do all of that texting—I can't see your facial expression and hear your tone of voice through no durn text. That's how people can hide how they feel or what they're going through, behind a text. I'm still your mama, I don't care how old you are! You better pick up the phone and call!" Silence.

"So, how come my grandbaby still got them braces on?"

"Um, that's what I was gonna ask you." Celeste bit her lip. She glanced at the phone screen and then reverted her eyes back to the road. "It's your birth month, right? With your book club? I was gonna ask you, see if I could hold a couple of dollars until my tax money comes in."

"TAX MONEY!! It's the end of May! What—"

"I know, I know, I know, but listen. It's fine. I let my friend claim Toot on her taxes this year. She already has two kids, so she'll get more money with Toot than I would with just one child. So, she said she would give me $4,000 back from the tax return. But the IRS is holding her check for some reason. She said she should have it in a few more weeks. As soon as she gets it, I can give you your money back. That's the money that I was going to use to pay the orthodontist bill. They won't take the braces off until I make the last payment."

Ruth was incredulous. "Celeste! The government released those tax refunds on February the twenty-first! It. Is. Almost. June! I bet you a dollar to a doughnut, that girl done spent every bit of that money. You'll never see it. I can't believe you did that!"

"Mama! Why you always yelling? She texted me the other day and said it should be here in a few weeks. I can handle it. But I need to get my baby's braces off before the eighth-grade formal, so are you gonna let me borrow the money? But don't put it in my account! It's in the negative so the bank will take it. You can just Western Union it." Celeste smiled into the phone screen. "Come on, Mama. Don't do Baby Toot like this."

Ruth sucked her teeth, stared into the phone. Celeste made her so durn mad, but there was nothing that she wouldn't do for her only grandbaby. "I'll send it the end of the week. And you better send it back. ASAP."

She pressed the red button on the phone screen.

Inside the trailer, she tried to go about her normal routine of showering, doing some laundry, and then dinner, but she felt unsettled. She hadn't really been comfortable since she moved in. She had taken every possible safety precaution, hoping that a sense of physical security might bring her some peace. The doors and locks had been reinforced. A monitored security system had been installed. Tonight, her uneasiness had nothing to do with feeling unsafe.

She sat on the couch and called her daughter back.

Celeste answered on the first ring. "Hey, Mama!"

"Um, look baby. I can't give you that money. I know I said I would, but it just doesn't sit right with me. You won't be able to pay me back, and I can't afford to lose any money. I want Toot to get her braces off, but I'm trying to manage my money differently, and I need you to start making wiser choices too. I have other obligations, other commitments, and—"

"That's cool. Don't even worry about us. We gonna be alright." Ruth scarcely recognized Celeste's frigid voice. The abruptness surprised her. By the time she collected her thoughts, her daughter had hung up.

Lying on the couch, she didn't even try to sleep. Insomnia chased away all the comfort that she should have enjoyed in the place she now called home. Even with her hammer and Bible within close reach, her restlessness was unabated. Still, she was waking up, adrenaline vibrating through her limbs, a caged bird flapping in her chest. It was surprising that she was even home tonight. Normally, she busied herself in every sense: prayed more, read more, walked more, went to the Y more, worked more. She picked up as many sitter shifts as possible, as much to avoid being home alone as it was to earn more money. Tonight, rather than sleep, her goal was to simply watch a few episodes of *The Golden Girls* until it was time to leave for the sitter shift.

When she stepped off of the elevator that evening, she could hear *him*. He was moaning, cursing the nurses, complaining that they were killing him.

"Miss Ruth, I am so, so sorry!" The lead night nurse was rushing toward her, whisper-shouting. "We were hoping that he would have been asleep by now, so that you wouldn't really have to deal with him. That way, you could just sit in there while he was asleep. If I had known

... well we still needed you because you're the only one-to-one who's on shift tonight ... but, I'm just sorry. They're sedating him now, so hopefully he'll go on to sleep and quit harassing everyone."

Ruth stood there in the hall, deciding on the best action to take in this situation. "It's alright. I can handle him. It's not like he's my husband anymore, right? He's just another patient." She produced a smile to let the nurses know that she appreciated their concern, then walked into his room and stopped dead in her tracks. The room smelled like fresh, raw feces. Ripe and strong.

A CNA was in the room, getting him settled into the bed. She rushed past Ruth, arms full of soiled sheets. "Code Brown! CODE BROWN! He just crapped the bed! I.

Cannot. Believe this!"

The aide's disgust should have humored Ruth, but the feeling that showed up instead was embarrassment. Embarrassment at having chosen such an animal for a mate one that she couldn't get rid of, even in divorce.

He was gross, yes. Mean, yes. But he hadn't always been that way. Once, in another lifetime, he had been her boyfriend. That idea sounded unbelievable now, but she wanted the nurses to know that he had been a good choice back then. She couldn't explain the guy that was lying in the bed tonight.

She didn't speak to him when she entered the stinking room, just began arranging her belongings in the corner and steadying herself with a pre-shift, humble prayer. She thanked God for delivering her from the abusive and dysfunctional marriage, told him that she trusted him in all ways, even the ways that she couldn't yet understand, asked him to heal her patient according to his holy will, and begged him, if the patient was not to be healed tonight, to at least let him fall fast asleep, that they might both find peace tonight.

"I didn't ask for no visitors! I don't want you in here! You didn't care about me before, don't be in here trying to care about me now!" He drooled the last words, the sedatives clearly taking effect on his consciousness but not his still spiteful spirit. He would be asleep soon.

Ruth continued to arrange her books, sweater, water bottle, and suddenly she was moving in reverse, packing up her things, getting her sweater on. Her arms and legs were buzzing with electricity as though she were just waking up, but she was wide awake.

In a step and a half, she was at his bedside, leaning over the pillow to speak directly into his ear. His body odor infuriated her. "You listen here. I did care for you, took care of you, and made excuses for you for a whole lot longer than you deserved. But I don't owe you anything anymore, don't have to do nothing for you! I don't have to put up with your … *this*, tonight or any other night."

She straightened up, turned to leave the room, but doubled back. "I don't have to put up with your damn shit." She never cursed, and she knew that her delivery was clumsy, but that didn't lessen the impact of her words. Her choice of words stunned him, too, his facial expression screwed into a combination of delirium and confusion. She knew him well, knew that he was genuinely confused about what he'd done wrong, that he really thought she had been there just to visit him.

Standing back, she evaluated her ex-husband's bitter and pathetic existence. True, he had not always been this abhorrent and barbaric. In the early years, she remembered that he liked to have fun, could entertain the nieces and nephews, worked hard to support the family. But, maybe, if she dug below the surface and exposed the real truth, the spitefulness, the harshness, the meanness had always been there.

She'd always known, had always wanted to believe, that there was a good person beneath the bear's facade that he wore, but now she questioned her judgement. The surly and cantankerous spirit that she tried to overlook had bubbled to the surface like a cancerous lesion. She watched his head bob and then settle into the pillow as saliva pooled at the corners of his lips. The sedatives had forced him to sleep against his will. She shook her head, disappointed that she had wasted her life on this.

Turning toward the dry-erase communication board that hung on the wall facing his bed, she left a message that would greet him when he awoke: *Rudeness is the weak man's imitation of strength.*

When she rounded the corner and stepped into the hallway, she was standing face-to-face with the CNAs and a few of the nurses. The charge nurse whispered, "You better go 'head, Miss Ruth! I've never, *ever* heard you curse before! You even sound nice when you're mad!" High-fives and laughter abounded.

Ruth headed home again. But the joke was on her when she arrived at home. Insomnia, the uninvited guest, had waited up for her. She laid on the couch again, looking at her Bible by the blue light of the television. She couldn't see the words clearly, but she knew most of it by heart anyway. It was entirely possible that she hadn't slept in her bed even once since she had moved into the trailer.

Actually, it was the absolute truth. It was a beautiful new bed, a housewarming gift from her daughter. Celeste had done the whole bedroom for her; curtains, a brand-new set of bedroom furniture, a deluxe bed-in-a-bag, lots of pillows, pictures, candles—she'd obviously spent money that she didn't have. It was a perfect room for someone else.

Ruth tucked the Bible between herself and the back of the couch, then flipped around toward the television. She shoved one hand under her pillow, greeting her old friend the hammer, then pulled the blanket up over her shoulder and secured it under her chin.

CHAPTER TWENTY

R uth's granddaughter, Toot, was in the backseat of Granddaddy Fields' old Buick Skylark, on the passenger's side. Ruth sat up front, riding shotgun, listening to him tell them stories about his younger days. He loved to take them on long drives and entertain them with his colorful stories.

Today, as he drove, he was telling them a story about how he'd once been given a beaten-up old motorcycle in exchange for doing some handiwork. He told them how he had brought the old chopper back to life. How he changed out the motor, painted it. How he never pulled it out of the garage but had simply loved working on it.

Toot, bored by the conversation, interrupted the story and began drilling Granddaddy with trivia questions.

"Granddaddy! What's the capital of California?" "Granddaddy! How many players are on a standard rugby team?" "What time is it in Italy?" "Who was the seventeenth President of the United States?"

Granddaddy, not knowing the answers, but intrigued by the game, threw out his best guesses. He watched in the rearview mirror, waiting for Toot to tell him if his answers were correct or incorrect.

With each incorrect answer, the little girl rolled down the car window and tossed a penny out. "Wrong answer! That's going to cost you!"

She taunted the elderly man mercilessly with questions that he couldn't possibly answer. "How many inches are in a mile?" "What size shoe does Michael Jordan wear?" "Where is the Sea of Tranquility located?"

Upon realizing that the girl was throwing money out of the window—literally throwing money away—Granddaddy became visibly upset. Not wanting to steal the child's apparent joy, but distraught by the sight of money being thrown away, he could barely concentrate on the road.

"Which civil rights' leader had the most missing teeth?" "How long can a lightning bug survive in an empty Coke bottle?" "What is the average length of a strand of human DNA?"

As Granddaddy floundered, the game became too uncomfortable for Ruth to watch. "Okay. Alright. That's enough." She tried to intervene, to get back to the motorcycle story. To return Granddaddy's attention to the road. But the girl continued to torment, drilling the old man with trivia. By now, she was tossing handfuls of pennies out of the window.

Granddaddy, right arm flailing about in the airspace between the front seat and the back seat, was pleading with the girl to stop throwing money out. To stop with the questions.

"They're just pennies," the girl chided. She was laughing and holding the coins just out of the old man's reach.

"They are not just pennies! That is money, and it adds up!" The old man was halfway in the backseat now, having turned and wedged himself between the drivers' and passengers' seats. Ruth was screaming hysterically, trying to take hold of the steering wheel, grabbing at her granddaddy's shirt, pulling him toward his seat.

The car veered furiously across the roadway, coming dangerously close to the railing that was supposed to prevent vehicles from driving off the side of the bridge, and it was picking up speed. She noticed that the gas pedal was pressed to the floor beneath the weight of her grandfather's foot as he stretched his body in a desperate effort to get into the backseat. The sound of gravel flying into the wheel wells and pinging the underside of the car grew louder as the vehicle skirted the edge of the road.

"Pennies aren't real money!" Toot was hollering. "You should know that since you're so smart!"

Ruth was turned around in her seat now, wanting to grab the little girl by the throat, but was unable to lift and extend her arms. The weight of her arms was tremendous, as thick and as heavy as sandbags.

Ruth jolted awake, heated by the vibrating adrenaline that coursed through her body. Her arm had fallen asleep and was still shoved under her pillow, smashed awkwardly against the hammer. Immediately surveying her surroundings, she recognized that she was at home— her home.

There was a text message from Julene: *Got my car back. Got rid of the loser. TTYL.*

The clock on the cable box read 4:15.

Okay, Lord. I'm up.

She was at the gym early enough to catch a spin class, a core strengthening mini boot camp, and then finish out with a five-mile run on the treadmill. Ruth wasn't a formally trained runner, but, other than prayer, she'd found that exercise had always been the best way to cope with her insidious anxiety.

Coming out of the locker room after showering, she bumped into Cynthia. "Hey! I see you're sticking to this fitness thing, huh?"

Cynthia shifted her duffle bag from one shoulder to the other and grinned at Ruth. "I know you work out more than an Olympic athlete! I'm just trying to get to your level one day!"

The two fell into step, crossing the parking lot that separated the hospital from the Y. Ruth glanced at Cynthia, able to see that her spandex pants and tank top revealed a trimmer figure. "But look at you! You've lost some weight, haven't you?"

Cynthia smiled and shrugged her shoulders. "I'm trying. I feel like I hit a plateau and I'm not even close to where I want to be. I'm not giving up though!"

Ruth checked her out, exaggerating her head and eye movements from Cynthia's head to her feet, front and back. "You better watch out! You gonna wind up with a man if you keep this up!"

They were laughing, and Cynthia pretended to cover her private parts, jokingly modest. "What kind of man wants an old maid who still lives with her mama?"

But when they stopped laughing, Cynthia eyed Ruth sideways. "I do want one though. A man, I mean. I know you just went through a bad situation, but I just keep hoping that I could find someone for me. I keep hoping that, with so much divorce and cheating out there, that there is still just one man for me. I still want a family."

She turned to Ruth, stopped walking. "Does that sound crazy? Am I crazy for trying to believe in a man? Or for wanting to have kids this late in life?"

Ruth grabbed her hand and pulled her along. "There's nothing crazy about that. You got your mind and your heart set on what you want. You just check with God and make sure that your wants are lined up with his will, and that you trust him to bring you together with the man that he has prepared for you." She squeezed Cynthia's hand gently. "Now, you might get in trouble if you try to make the Lord's will line up with the man that you think you want, but you'll never go wrong when you recognize the man that is already aligned with his will. See? Don't get it twisted. And don't look at my life as an example. That has nothing to do with what's in store for yours."

"I'm trying to hold on to that. Trying to stay positive like you. Because, I'm being honest here, it's not looking too good. I've made some bad choices. I've gained all this weight. I have my mom to take care of. Sometimes, I wonder if it's too late for all of it—the kids and everything. When we started in with the savings thing and reading the financial stuff, talking about establishing something for our children, a little piece of me was thinking to myself, *'Are you even having children? Can you even have babies?'*"

She straightened up, squeezed Ruth's hand, and swung it back and forth. "But I had to pray against that! Asked God to show me something else, tell me something different. I started thinking about how, in one of our financial books, they talked so much about knowing what you want and training your mind to think positive. And how he broke down the six ghosts of fear."

Ruth nodding in agreement, loving the spirits of hope and faith that had energized Cynthia, and attempted to offer a thought. "You know, you can find those same principles in the Bible ..."

"You know what God told me, Ruth? He said, 'Girl, save your money, build that foundation, so you can afford to get your mama some in-home health care and you can visit some faraway places!' Maybe my future husband is in Italy!" Cynthia was laughing. "Maybe he's running his family's business in Dubai. How would we ever meet if I don't get up out of this place sometime?"

They were both laughing by now. Cynthia scanned the half-empty parking lot, sweeping her hand across the whole place. "I don't see my Arabian prince anywhere around here! You seen him? You hiding him in there somewhere?" She patted Ruth's pockets, searching playfully.

"I haven't seen him. I promise I would tell you!" Ruth held her empty hands up. "But if you find him—when you find him—let me know if he has an older brother. Or a younger one, for that matter!"

Ruth stood at the entrance of the closet where she and Irene kept their lab coats and disposables likes caps, gloves, and biohazard gowns. Unable to find her glasses and thinking that she must have left them in the pocket of one of her other jackets, she fished around in the pockets of each jacket hanging on the rack.

When Irene walked in, reached past her in the closet, and grabbed her own jacket without saying a word, Ruth waited for the bomb to drop. A quiet Irene was like the calm before the storm. Ruth stood near the closet, buttoning her own lab coat silently, and waited for it.

Jacket on, but unbuttoned, Irene disappeared into the closet again and reappeared with two disposable shoe covers. She handed one to Ruth. Leaning against the wall, she took her glasses off and rubbed her face.

Ruth used her foot to push a chair closer to her friend, but Irene shook her head. "I can't sit down. My back is killing me already this morning."

Searching gingerly for the right words, Ruth tried a different approach. "Did you hear about—"

"You know, Lord knows I have tried with my sons! Both of them! It's like they just won't do right! It's like they're stuck on 'stupid'. Can't get right. And I don't know what else to do for them. That oldest one ... honey, he ..." Irene was venting to herself as much as she was to Ruth. She paused for a moment, struggling to get the thin, blue cap over her hair. "... he just irks my nerve sometimes! I put the money in his account because he said the kids needed some school clothes, and this joker done went and spent the money on a needle for some turntable he done bought from somewhere. Talking about how he gonna start deejaying parties! Spent three

…" She yanked the cap off, flipped it around and tried it on again. "Spent $300 on a record player needle! Three-oh-five, ninety-nine, to be exact." Sensing that there was more, Ruth sat down.

"And Nathaniel. My Nate." The disappointment and sadness in Irene's voice foreshadowed the story. "That boy gave the cat to some guy that he met on the internet who said he could mate it. Didn't know this guy from Adam! And you can just guess what happened!" She didn't wait for Ruth to guess. "The guy disappeared with the cat. Just fell off the face of the earth, I guess. And now Dee-Dee done kicked him out for being stupid. And I don't blame her. So, guess who came knocking on my door last night?!" Frustrated with the cap that wouldn't fit on her head, she pulled it off again and sat next to her old friend.

"What am I supposed to do? Honey, I can't make this stuff up! Why would he do that?" She laughed a little. "What he did was about as dumb as the boy in the book about the Babylon people. The one who gave his gold coins away to some con artist and lost his life savings."

Ruth stood up and snapped her fingers. "That's it! That's exactly what he sounds like! How crazy is it that we just read about it? When I got to that part, I thought it sounded like something *my* daughter would do." Hand on hip, she asked Irene the million-dollar question, "So, what did you do?"

Irene walked over to the mirror and tried again to force the cap onto her head. "I let him in. He had my grandbabies standing there with their little sleeping bags and everything! I just opened the door, and let them in. I took the kids in the room with me and let them get in my bed, and I just closed my room door on him. Ain't no telling how long they'll be staying with me." She threw the cap down on the floor, tried to kick it, but the thin piece of fabric just fluttered in the air, propelled by the wind from her moving foot.

Ruth leaned into the closet and pulled out two bouffant caps, placing one over her own hair, passing the other to Irene.

"Thanks, honey. I don't know what was wrong with that other one."

Looping her arm through Irene's, Ruth led her toward the computer. "It was a shoe cover. You clean or dirty today?

CHAPTER TWENTY-ONE

As the presiding officer, Irene volunteered to host the next club meeting at her house. The undertaking, though it would have been sufficient under normal circumstances, paled in comparison to Cynthia's recently flamboyant events. Irene had done her best though, and the table was set with a fruit and cheese platter, Ritz crackers, chicken wings, a pan of her famous macaroni and cheese, and a jug of lemonade.

"Hey! Y'all come on in! And don't judge me! I didn't know that the hosting would be so much work, or we would have had it at Cynthia's house again!" Irene greeted her guests with the candor and light-heartedness of a late-night comedian. She held the screen door open for everyone. "Come on in and just step right over my son. Nathaniel! Get up off the steps so people can get in!"

Closing his laptop and stepping down off the front steps, Nathaniel ushered the women in. "Welcome to our humble home, ladies." He bowed and imitated a doorman. "Right this way. Right this way."

Irene welcomed her friends as they filed in, cheek-to-cheek kissing and hugging warmly. "Ignore him, y'all. How is he gonna welcome people to *our* home when he's a guest too?"

Irene's living room wasn't as spacious as Cynthia's home, but she had done her best to accommodate everyone.

Children's toys were piled in one corner, and metal folding chairs were lined up in rows in the center of the living room, facing a white sheet that was pinned to the wall with thumbtacks. "Come on in! Come on in and have a seat! I have a little something special in store for you!"

When everyone had found a seat, Irene brought the meeting to order through prayer. *"Lord. Thank you for all that you have done for us. We have much work to do, and we need you, God. We need your hand on us, we need you here in this place with us tonight, God. To show us what to do. To help us along the way. And we ask you to speak to us, Holy Spirit. Because we know that books are just pages with words until you anoint them, Lord. Only you can make it all make sense. Only you can help us to apply this knowledge in a way that benefits your kingdom and your children. And we are so thankful, Lord, for the way that you hold us all together. Lord, there's been no fussing, no fighting, but Lord, you have drawn us closer to one another. You have turned us into a family and we are excited about what you have in store for us. Thank you for continuing to bless us in ways that we could not even imagine. We bless your son's glorious name, and we say amen. Amen. And amen."*

Following her earnest prayer, Irene's pious expression transitioned to a bright smile as she moved to the evening's topic of discussion. "Well, we read a pretty interesting book, and I don't know about you all, but I can say that I actually enjoyed it. I finished it in one weekend, and I even took notes. I put this slide show together, and by

'I', I mean my grandbaby, MacKenzie." She lowered the window shades and turned the lights off, then shouted down the hallway, "Kenzie!"

In seconds, MacKenzie bounced into the living room, tutu skirt and ponytails swirling, and a blue light appeared in the center of the white sheet. Irene was beaming. "Kenzie setup this projector, y'all. All I had to do was tell her what to put on it! Kids these days! Amazing!"

The music from Dora the Explorer began playing, and then: *"Pea-nut butta jell-lay! Pea-nut butta jell-lay! Peanutbutta-jelly-Peanut-butta-jelly-Peanut-butta-jelly-with-abaseball-bat!"* The hip hop music was blasting and words flashed onto the sheet:

> *Eight Things You Should Have Learned from this Reading Selection:*
>
> *Pay yourself first. (Fatten your purse.)*
>
> *Live below your means. (Stop spending so much!)*
>
> *It takes money to make money. (Invest but choose wisely!)*
>
> *Get insurance. (Protect your investments, protect your family.)*
>
> *Treat your home as an investment. (The landlord is not your friend! Be a homeowner.)*
>
> *Plan for your retirement. (Embrace the concept of compound interest to keep the money flowing.)*

> *Invest in yourself. (Learn more to earn more.)*
>
> *Track your wealth. (Know where you are but keep your eyes on the prize.)*

In the last slide, Dora and Boots hovered mid-air, celebrating with a high-five, and the thumping music ended abruptly. When the lights came on, Irene was standing next to MacKenzie with a look of overwhelming pride. "Y'all give my baby a hand! She's too smart for the second grade, isn't she? Ain't no way in the *world* that I could have made something like that by myself!" MacKenzie was smiling too. She had no front teeth, but was clearly pleased with herself, and the room erupted into applause.

MacKenzie was excused and Irene continued. "If anyone would like a copy of our featured presentation, MacKenzie will have to show me how to email the link to you. Don't judge me, I'm still learning this computer stuff! Okay. Let's move on. Julene, do you have any updates for us?"

Julene stood. "Well that was very entertaining, wasn't it?" She grinned at her friends. "Actually, I think that MacKenzie has a future in the audio-visual field, so let's make sure that she can afford to go to college to pursue it. Last time we met, we voted on our leaders, and we decided to read this book, which I really loved. Irene apparently got a lot out of it too. What'd y'all think?"

Ruth looked around the room. "I don't know about y'all, but it had so many thy's, thee's, thine's, and ye's that I thought I was reading the Old Testament!"

Irene laughed out loud. "As much as you read the Bible, that should have made you feel right at home!" Laughter and giggling filtered through the room.

Julene, struggling to speak through her own laughter, agreed with Ruth. "Right. Right. The language was definitely from the Jesus days, but I thought it was really good information. I kind of wish someone had taught me those lessons a *long* time ago. That's the kind of stuff they should have been teaching in the schools, instead of boring us to death with all of that Shakespeare and whatnot."

"True that!" Cynthia scooted to the edge of her seat. "That part about saving a percentage of your earnings, oh my God! When I started calculating how much I could have saved at just 10 percent, it made me feel sick to my stomach. But I like the way the old man always reminded the boy that he could start again after he lost everything. You know, if you make a bad decision, you just learn from it and start again."

"To God be the glory. Isn't he the God of a second chance!" Julene lifted her hands in praise before continuing. "And why shouldn't you put aside a portion of everything you earn? Pay your tithes, give an offering, but pay yourself too. But the way that he worded it in the book, it made a lot more sense—keeping a portion of everything that you earn doesn't mean saving some money to pay the bill collector or get your nails done. Keeping it for yourself means *keeping it for yourself*. You know you're gonna pay the landlord and the car note every month like clockwork, make a decision to pay yourself too. One coin at a time."

Monica raised her hand and then pointed at her own chest. "I know, at least for me, I always end up making do with whatever I have. For instance, if my check is short, or somebody messes up my automatic draft, or the gas station decides to put a hold on $250 of my money for up to three business days," she looked around and received a few fist bumps, "everything always works out in the end. I guess that's what the author meant when he talked about getting along just as fine on nine coins as he used to get along on ten. Then, when his little purse started filling up with his savings, he noticed that the money seemed to be coming to him even easier." Her eyes brightened, even as she was speaking, and she asked the ladies a serious question: "Do you really believe what the old man was saying? That you can attract money to yourself?"

Scooting her chair around to see everyone's faces, Ruth shared a confession. "Well, after reading this particular book, I decided to quit putting money in the nurse's lottery pool at work. In my reading, it was my understanding that there is a difference between good luck and good fortune. I'm training myself to stop saying that I need to get lucky and win the lottery. Seems like I'll have a better chance of good fortune from working harder at making better choices with my time and money. Think y'all," she paused to collect everyone's attention. "Think about what he said. Some people do get lucky— they hit the number or whatever—but they can't hold on to it. They usually end up broke again. But, just ask a group of successful people how they got so wealthy, and I'd bet you that not a one of them would tell you they got rich off of a scratch-off ticket or a bingo game."

Irene, who was gathering empty plates, straightened up and put one hand on her hip. "So, you're telling me that winning the lottery isn't a good retirement plan?" A barely suppressed smile played at the corners of her lips.

"Well, *you* can put your money on a racehorse or a slot machine in Atlantic City, but I'm putting mine over there in that savings account until I can put it on something that I *know* will win!" Elisha put one hand on her hip to mirror Irene, but she failed in her attempt to maintain a straight face. "So, I think that we need to just follow these lessons and keep on saving our little coins like the book said."

Julene jumped up, pretending to referee the two women. "Okay. Anyways." She referred back to her notebook, "Let's stay on track before we get ourselves in trouble! Cynthia informed us that we had saved $6,000 at our last meeting. How much do we have now, Madam Treasurer?"

Cynthia referred to her notebook. "We have $7,200 as of last payday."

"Alright," Julene wrote the number down and flipped a page in her own notebook. "Now, the next book on our list is one that deals with the psychology of money and should help us to focus on creating life experiences rather than focusing on accumulating material things. When we last spoke, I told her that our goal wasn't necessarily to get rich, it was to be financially independent and smarter about the way that we manage and spend our money, so that's what she recommended." Julene looked toward Irene, signaling the end of her report.

Irene stood up and addressed her friends in a loud whisper that was clearly meant to be overheard by Julene.

"She can speak for herself! I'm trying to be rich!" She glanced over at Julene and then burst out laughing. "I'm just kidding! You actually made a good point—you got to be careful about idolizing money. The Book of Timothy talks about that. So, thank you for what you're doing, Julene. All those in favor of the next book selection, say 'aye.' All who are opposed, say 'nay.'" The 'ayes' had it.

Chapter Twenty-Two

A teal blue sticky note fluttered out of Ruth's locker when she opened the door. The swirly, girly, neon pink letters were entirely too fancy for the subject matter: *Signature on form when you get a sec.*

She stuck her head in Cynthia's office, her eyebrow and the sticky note raised in solidarity.

"Oh!" Cynthia flipped through a stack of papers and envelopes in her desk drawer and pulled out an envelope with a form paper-clipped to the front. "So, I guess they want you to sign off here—" she pointed to the signature line at the bottom of the form, "—saying that you received this benefits information. Apparently, since you were grandfathered in from the old benefits program, your employee pension plan and stocks have to be rolled over into something else. When we discussed this last time, you rolled your pension into the 401(k)."

Ruth rolled her eyes. "If that's what you want to call it. After paying the divorce attorney and putting the down-payment on the trailer, there's barely anything else left! I got the account statement the other day. Thirty-five hundred dollars left. I can't even afford to get old on that money."

Cynthia nodded knowingly. "Let me tell you something. After everything that I've learned from helping my mom with her affairs, you're right. That social security money and all the taxes that come out of your paycheck ... the government makes it so hard for you to get it by the time you need it. And the little bit that they give you isn't enough to live on. If you manage to have a little bit of money of your own, if you have *any* assets, then they reduce your benefits even more. But don't even get me started on that stuff."

She tapped the envelope on the desk. "They're saying that you still need to make a decision about the other part. It keeps coming down to these shares that you received as part of your compensation package years ago." She looked at Ruth for a long moment. "How did that happen anyway? They don't even do that anymore. From what I heard, they basically did it just for you."

Ruth thought back to her early years as a hospital employee. "When I first came into Central Sterile Supply, I didn't know what I was walking into. There were probably twenty to thirty items missing from the case carts every day! It was an unorganized mess down there. The old team had been fired right before I was hired—I guess the hospital was receiving complaints from the surgeons about the instrument flow—and the Central Sterile manager was looking to bring in a consultant. Things got so bad that the surgeons stopped requesting privileges in this hospital. No surgeon wanted to work here. We had such a bad reputation." She shook her head, remembering all the confusion.

"The hospital was going to pay thousands of dollars to this consultant. They called it Lean Consulting. They were going to pay this company thousands of dollars to do a two-week study to figure out why the department was running so inefficiently. Then they were going to implement a five-month plan to make the improvements. And that was going to cost around $100,000! Actually, I think it might have been even more than that."

Nodding, Cynthia leaned forward and spoke in a hushed voice. "I believe it! You would not believe some of the stuff the hospital spends money on! Meanwhile, they say they can't afford to pay us more money."

Ruth smirked. "Well, the crazy thing is, I could see what was wrong down there after my first week on the job! My *first* week! You didn't need to be a consultant to figure it out. First of all, too many people from the OR were coming down, pulling instruments for the carts. I mean, four or five people a day were coming in there messing with stuff. Then, they were making the carts too far in advance, so they didn't have the instruments that they needed for today because those instruments were sitting on tomorrow's cart! I'm looking at them like, 'You can't hoard no instruments and keep other people from using them!' We just don't have enough instruments for that.

"So, what happened was, the nurses and surgical techs were tipping down there and stealing items from carts that were already prepped, but they weren't replacing them. Then, when the surgeons asked for something, it wasn't on the cart. Now, you gotta waste time, interrupt a surgery, and run around looking for this and that! They would come running down into my department all in a panic, looking for instruments, disturbing *me* and stressing *me* out! Didn't make a bit of sense!

"Supplies were all over the place, nurses were hoarding their own supplies—my nerves couldn't take it. So, I cut them off from coming into my department all times of the day and night. I organized all the hard and soft supplies. Then, I gave the OR techs a set time to come down and pull their soft goods and get everything that they needed at one time. After that we would pull the equipment and instruments for the carts and put it all together. We started sending the first two carts upstairs for the next day and I held the rest of the carts in Central Sterile until they were ready for them. In the morning, I let the nurse come in and verify that she had what she needed on the carts and that's it."

Ruth leaned against the doorway of Cynthia's office, still amazed that the department had been so unorganized back then. "Then I had them to bring Irene in to work with me. They had her on the janitorial team, and I knew she didn't want to be pushing that mop for the rest of her life!"

"Ruth! I'm not kidding! They pay people big bucks to come in and turn an entire department around like that! There's no telling how much money you saved them. I guess that's why they awarded you with the additional compensation."

"Well they could have kept this Wall Street foolishness and just given me some cash instead!"

"Too late to do anything about it, now. So here, take it with you and read it over." Cynthia handed the envelope to Ruth, who looked over the document. It could have just as well been written in Arabic—she didn't understand any of it.

At home that night, sufficiently settled in on the couch, she pulled the paper out of the envelope and looked it over. Issued by a company called CompuShare, it detailed an employee investment and reinvestment program. Words like dividend, direct registration, certificated shares, reinvesting dividends, and closing price per share peppered the page. She closed her eyes and prayed that the words would be translated from gibberish to English when she opened them again. They were not.

She looked at the form again, flipping it over, searching for a legend or any additional information that would help her to take the appropriate action. There was nothing. Having read a few books, now, on self-improvement and wealth building, she was no expert, not by any imaginative contortion, but she had learned one theme which seemed to be consistent among most of the books: seek wise counsel. Consult an expert for help in the areas where you are inexperienced or less knowledgeable.

She dialed the CompuShare customer service number.

CHAPTER TWENTY-THREE

Elisha and Julene met Ruth in the parking lot after work. Julene was the first to speak. "Got a little problem. Apparently, Monica wants to withdraw her money and leave the club. Somebody said she—never mind never mind, here she comes."

Ruth looked up to see Monica coming toward them. "Okay, wait a minute! Come on, y'all! Monica! What are they talking about? You leaving?"

Monica walked over and leaned against the car, exhaling heavily. "I can't do the club anymore. My husband found out about it—I was using the minutes from the last meeting as a bookmark and he found it. Said we can't afford to be wasting money on a bootleg investment club. I know we have bills, but we have to plan for our future too. For the kids' futures. My baby girl will be driving next year, and she'll be in college before we know it! My son is right behind her, and now we have my nephew staying with us too. But he wants me to get my money back and quit the club."

The women stood speechless, looking at one another, dumbstruck.

"Nope. Not gonna do it." Ruth grabbed hold of Monica's hand and pulled her into a hug as she spoke.

"Naw, baby, I know that's your husband, but you're one of us. If *you* wanted to go, if *you* felt that it wasn't right for you, then I could see it, but for *him* to force you—that's a controlling spirit. It isn't godly."

The other ladies closed in and joined hands, strengthening the circle.

Monica wiped away hot tears with the sleeve of her sweater. "I don't want to do it, y'all know that. I prayed and prayed about this thing last night, and I know we're doing the right thing. But my husband just doesn't see it. I thought about just doing it anyway, just putting in my money without telling him like I was doing before, but he's watching me like a hawk now. He was online checking my bank account this morning."

Irene and Cynthia walked up and joined the circle.

"Whoa! Whoa! What's going on here?" Irene burst right into the center of the group, eyes searching her friends' faces. Ruth spoke. "Monica's husband is making her quit the club. He told her to get her money back."

Irene stepped in front of Monica and looked straight into her eyes. "But what do *you* want?"

"I don't want to quit."

Irene stepped back, smiling, "Okay, then you don't quit. If anybody knows about working around a husband, it's me! Honey, they don't know a thang! They just like to *feel* like they running something. Look, this is what you do: tell him that you put in the request to get your money back—it's gonna take a while to process, though, because you know, it'll take five to seven business days for the bank to do it. Who knows? It might take longer than that!" she nudged Monica and smiled slyly.

"That'll make him feel like you followed his 'orders'. Then," she looked over at Cynthia, "Cynthia, you just change that payroll so that you can split her direct deposit. Take out her fifty dollars from each check and have them cut a live check for it. Put that check into our account. The rest can go to her direct deposit so that he can 'see' her pay go in if he starts feeling like he wants to check up on her again."

A slow clap began within the circle and the ladies bowed down comically to Irene as though she were royalty. "Look y'all. I'm not a liar, but sometimes you gotta play the game with these men. Keep them quiet and still handle your business! One monkey don't stop no show! We started this thing together—the Lord done already put His blessing on it—and we're gonna finish together! Now can I get an amen to that?"

As Ruth headed toward her car, Julene caught up with her, gently pulling at the back of her sleeve to slow her down.

"You going home? Mind if I catch a ride with you?"

Ruth shook her head. "Not today. Gotta hot date. Sorry."

Realizing that Julene was no longer walking alongside her, Ruth stopped and turned around. Julene, standing stock still, was speechless.

"Just kidding! I'm kidding! You know I don't have a boyfriend. Yeah, you can ride with me!"

Inside the car, Julene played with the radio, changing the stations until she found one she liked. "Thanks for the ride. I feel like I'm always asking you for something. I let my little cousin hold my car and she's supposed to be at a job interview right now. I moved her into the house with me and the kids since I kicked their father out. Apparently, he's in rehab now."

Switching the radio back to contemporary gospel, Ruth nodded. "That sounds good. Was it voluntary? The rehab?"

"Yeah, I guess you could say that. He was out there in the streets, and I heard that his mama got ahold of him and basically forced him to go, so …"

"Alright. Well that's better than nothing. Let's just continue to keep him in prayer, then. Maybe he can get himself together. And your cousin is helping with the kids?"

"Un-huh. She's a sweet girl and it helps her out too. She needed to get her life together and her family wasn't trying to help her. She keeps the kids when I'm at work, so I try to let her use my car to do things with them so they won't be stuck in the house all day. And she's taking some online courses. She had a job interview today with this company that's going to let her work from home taking calls for customer service."

"Okay," Ruth smiled at Julene, nodding her approval. "That sounds like a win-win for both of you. And for the children too."

"It is. She definitely helps me out, and I'm trying to help her out too. I've been talking to her about the books that we're reading, trying to kick some knowledge and get her into reading too. I keep telling her that she better get her life together or she's gonna end up just like me."

Ruth looked over at Julene, grabbed her hand and held it as she drove. "Ain't nothing wrong with you, Julene. The devil is a bold-faced liar."

CHAPTER TWENTY-FOUR

Hospital scrubs had become Ruth's signature outfit for meetings in the attorney's offices. Fortunately, she wasn't here for a divorce this time. She smiled at no one in particular, thinking that she'd probably seen the inside of an attorney's office as many times as Julene, by now.

The plush decor, mahogany-wood-everything, whisper-

quiet voices, suits, heels, papers, file folders, and even the smell of the attorney's office had become familiar. The smell of leather mixed with coffee beans offered a refreshing contrast to the scent of CaviCide and hot steam that filled her own workspace every day.

For help in deciphering the CompuShare statement, she was seated before Ahmir Bhimani, Esq. For an attorney, Ahmir looked young in Ruth's opinion, and spoke with the halting rhythm of a man for whom English was not the primary language. Taking in the dark-skinned Indian man's appearance, Ruth noted that he could have easily passed for a black guy—until he spoke. He cleared his throat a number of times prior to speaking, and Ruth determined that he was either nervous or unable to find the proper English translation for what he wanted to say.

Stalling. Papers were shuffled, tapped on the spotless desk, and then placed in a file folder. Reaching back inside the folder, he pulled out the CompuShare statement sheet and laid it on the desk, spinning it around so that both he and Ruth could read it together.

"Okay, Miss Ruth. I will first explain—well, essentially—" his finger darted across the paper, pointing from one item to another without forming a coherent sentence. "Okay, now—"

Ruth touched his hand, halting its frantic journey across the document. "Just tell me what they want me to do. I see that these are shares and not money, but it was part of the hospital's old pension plan and I know that means it goes toward retirement. So, how do I put this into my retirement? The hospital doesn't manage this part anymore, so I need to take care of it, and I don't need the IRS banging down my door because I did it wrong. What do you recommend?"

Ahmir stared at her, blinking, and Ruth noticed that his beautifully long, dark lashes smashed against the lenses of his glasses whenever his eyes moved.

I have someone that you need to meet. She might have said that out loud.

"Ma'am?"

She was immediately embarrassed. "I said, what do you recommend?"

Ahmir sat back now and smiled. With the tension broken, he found his words. "Miss Ruth, apparently your employers thought very highly of you during your early years at the hospital. Companies don't offer benefits like this anymore. They gave you a bunch of shares of their stock as part of your compensation package. And, as I said, this rarely happens anymore. I would guess that the shares were worth pennies back then. From the hospital's perspective, awarding you the shares was cheaper than giving you a raise, I imagine."

Ruth nodded, remembering the day she learned that she would be receiving shares in lieu of an annual raise, remembering that her husband was furious when she had come home and told the story. He had accused her of lying, had accused her of hiding money from him.

She nodded slowly. "Yes. Yes, I do remember that."

Ahmir, smiled again, gaining confidence. "Okay, these shares are worth substantially more now. Much more than they were when they were given to you."

Ruth smiled at him, beginning to understand. "Alright, well that makes sense. Stocks are supposed to go up in value and it was for retirement, so it was supposed to stay in there for a long time. Should I just cash it out and put it into the 401(k)? Is that an option? Or, is the government going to penalize me for cashing it? What are we talking about—

$400 or $500?"

Ahmir, for the first time, met Ruth's eyes directly. "Add a few hundred thousand dollars to that."

CHAPTER TWENTY-FIVE

R uth embarked on her daily run with a spirit of gratitude and mindfulness, as she did most days.

She ran with intention and acknowledged her appreciation for her legs, her muscles, her clear mind, her life. She acknowledged the fact that, for as long as she could remember, running had been the only way to calm the chaos in her chest. She was aware that, today, as she ran, she was weightless on her feet. Her muscles, her joints, and her breathing, all operated together in effortless harmony. The music that burst through her earbuds on most days was merely ambient on this day. She was wholly in tune with herself.

This must be the way that a runner's high feels. She had heard of it but couldn't recall a time in her life when she had experienced a moment such as this one—when all her senses were elevated with awareness, when nothing hurt.

The beauty, the peace, the euphoria of the moment brought tears to her eyes and, barely able to see through the tears, she stopped running. Without the steady crunch and thump of her sneaker soles gripping and releasing the asphalt, she found herself enveloped in an unfamiliar silence. Ruth wanted to run again, wanted to feel the high again, but was powerless in her attempts to move her own limbs.

Resigning herself to the moment, she released a cleansing breath and allowed her eyelids to close. In the absence of sight, her other senses moved to the forefront of her consciousness. She was smelling, feeling, hearing … she was in the space between the awakening and the opening of the eyes.

Remarkably, in the midst of that space—which simultaneously feels infinite and fleeting, there was no wild bronco bucking in her chest. For the first time— for the last time—Ruth rested in perfect peace.

EPILOGUE

The news of Ruth's sudden passing affected her friends in a way that mirrored the life she had lived. Quiet as it was, it struck them both quickly and slowly. The shock of their loss jolted them into an unpleasant consciousness. It disrupted the rhythm of their hearts. For them, a disturbance had been created from which they could not run. Instead, the ladies of the book club strengthened their resolve to fulfill the legacy that Ruth had believed in so fervently.

The book club meetings continued. The ladies had chosen a book that offered a slight break from the financial focus, turning their attention back toward personal enlightenment.

They agreed to read *The Alchemist*, although it forced them all to stray even further away from the comfort zone they had always enjoyed in literature.

"We can handle it," Irene had said when they were deciding whether to select it. "I mean, we just finished reading a book about a World War II fighter pilot! So, it's not like we're going to go back to reading mystery and romance novels anymore, anyway." And so, it had been decided.

Cynthia had chosen another, appropriately themed menu for the meeting. In honor of the novel's Middle Eastern setting, she prepared an assortment of Egyptian street foods. There was a type of Egyptian pizza— essentially a flaky pastry filled with cheese, chicken, and peppers. She had also tried her hand at falafel, stuffed peppers called mahshi, spicy rice with sausage, Arabic bread with tahini dip, a fruit and yogurt dessert called coctel, tea, and spiced coffee. The spread also included a pan of baked macaroni, courtesy of Irene.

When the women had greeted one another and filed into the dining room to admire the spread, they joined hands for the blessing. Tamara's voice filled the room, surprising everyone:

"Dear Lord! Oh, we come together this evening to bless your Holy name! Thank you for keeping us, Lord. You didn't have to do it, but you did! Thank you for guiding us, Lord. For your grace while we learn. Lord, we thank you for bringing us together, for the hedge of protection that surrounds us, for the way that you hold us up when we feel weak, Lord. We miss our sister Ruth, Lord. But your word says, 'to be absent from the body is to be present with the Lord.' It's been hard, dear God, but you sustain us, and we trust you. We believe you. So, we thank you, even tonight for the breath in our bodies, God. For the hands that prepared the food, Lord. For the safe place in which we are gathered tonight, Lord. May our bodies and minds be nourished in the way that you see most fitting for us, God, because you alone know what's best and we depend on you. In your precious son's Holy name, we all say amen."

Amens and murmurs of agreement flowed through the room, small plates were filled with foreign delicacies plus mac and cheese, and the women drifted into the living room to address the main order of the evening.

Cynthia stood in front of the group. "So … okay. I know this is going to feel a little different." She exhaled heavily and shook her hands out as though they were wet. "I hope everyone enjoyed *The Alchemist*—I know I did. And I feel like it was right on time for us. That's how God does it, right?" She smiled a little. "Right. But, instead of discussing the book tonight, we have a special guest." She extended a hand toward the woman who had been waiting patiently for the group to settle into place. "Ms. Saultina Dyer."

The tiniest applause trickled through the room as Tina made her way to the front of the group. Straightening her pants suit, she smiled.

"Hello, ladies. You can call me Tina. It is truly my pleasure to finally meet you! I have to say, when Julene contacted me and asked for my advice on your …" she searched for words. "When Julene told me what you all were wanting to do, I have to be honest. I was worried. It's not something that many people are able to pull off, whether we're talking about families or major corporations. When it comes to money—" she winked at the women, "you know how it can be. Even with the best intentions, things can get tricky. Relationships can be ruined. But you ladies— you have really come together to establish something that is phenomenal, and frankly, unprecedented. Establishing a corporate-style trust to protect and support your families, your future generations, is impressive and courageous.

"Now, if you'll have me as your advisor through the process, I want to make sure that you understand what this means, and I have some important advice for you. First, continue to educate yourselves, to empower yourselves in your decision-making. Also, plan to have regular meetings to monitor your trust's growth and progress. But, you can't do this alone. You don't want to build something that your family will destroy, and you don't want to build something that will destroy your family." She paused to allow her words time to sink in.

"So, you have to educate your families, mainly your children and grandchildren. Teach the little ones, your nieces and nephews, how to be fiscally responsible, how to save, because one day, Lord willing, they will be tasked with a great responsibility in managing this trust. They'll be making decisions for the fruits of your labor, if you will. Start training them up *today*. Teach them the sense of responsibility rather than entitlement.

"Alright." She fished through her briefcase and produced a stack of documents, referred to the top page. "Through the savings program that you all implemented early on, you managed to accrue a nice little nest egg to fund your trust. The money that you contributed as a group will be protected from bankruptcy, divorce, and certain tax liabilities, but it isn't necessarily enough to cover, say, a mortgage or a college tuition in a way that would yield any significant interest. In other words, if your goal is to save your money and use it to earn more money, then that would require a substantially larger contribution.

"Please accept my condolences on the loss of your friend Ruth. I had the pleasure of meeting her and she was a beautiful person. Truly inspiring, smart, and incredibly brave. Prior to her sudden passing, Ruth informed me that her intention was to augment the funds that you had saved as a group with the proceeds from the sale of her shares of Landis Memorial Hospital, a property currently held by the publicly traded Landis Vereen Healthcare Group. Her contribution increases the value of your trust fund by a total of $541,925."

Somewhere in the room, a teacup collided with the hardwood floor. Down the hall, the sound of Judge Mathis' voice blared from the television in Cynthia's mother's room.

"Now." Tina flipped the top sheet to the bottom of the pile and began handing out certificates that were printed on birch-colored, woven professional paper. "These are copies of the trust documents for your records. I have the rest here," she pointed at her briefcase, "which I would be happy to file for you if you would be so kind as to grant me the honor of serving as your trust attorney."

There, printed on the certificates, were the names of the trustees:

Ruthena Elaine Gentry

Irene Lee Arnold

Cynthia Yvette Thomas

Carolyn Julene Davis

Tamara Bernette Dudley

Elisha Evelina Johnson

Frankie Maye Minter

Tanisha Marie Allen

Emma Lee Howell

Monica Gibbs-Grant

Adriane Simone Vereen

Vermona Grace Arzate

Tina paused for the longest of moments, respectfully allowing time for the ladies to wrap their minds around the bombshell she had delivered. She knew from experience that a monetary windfall could be both a blessing and a burden. Inwardly, she wondered what would become of this group.

As the last of the tears were dried, as the last hands were clasped and released, as each pair of eyes turned toward Tina with a childlike expectancy, she concluded her visit with one final question. One that wouldn't be answered immediately:

"Ladies, the document that you hold represents a tremendous opportunity. What will you do with it?"

"Thanks for reading *Trust.*
If you'd like to stay in touch with me, join my newsletter and follow me on social media.
https://booksbydaines.com/pages/beta-and-book-clubs
https://twitter.com/booksbydaines
https://www.facebook.com/BooksbyDaines/
https://www.instagram.com/booksbydaines/

"If you enjoyed this story, check out this sneak peek of the next book in the *Trust* series. And please leave a review on Amazon.

SNEAK PEEK CHAPTER ONE

Four minutes. According to SavvyCrush.com, a woman should wait a minimum of four minutes before responding to a text from a man. That is, if she doesn't want to look too desperate.

This bit of info crosses my mind when I hear my iPhone text notification, which sounds like a perfect, single droplet of water. It causes me to stop wiping down the kitchen counter and glance at the clock on the stove. 8:19pm. From where I stand, I can see my phone screen become illuminated for a moment and then go dim, but I don't touch it.

To be clear, my waiting has nothing to do with desperation or the lack thereof-- I'm trying to train him-- assuming it *is* him-- to understand I'm not just sitting by the phone waiting for a text, and that's why I hold off for exactly seven minutes before checking the text message waiting, unopened on my phone.

I scrub at a nonexistent spot on the counter and move closer to the phone, but stick to my self-imposed waiting period. I won't pick it up or check to see who the text is from until 8:26.

Technically, I could check it now and still wait to reply. It's not like anyone would know. But I figure, if I can resist the urge to look at the message for a few more minutes, then somehow I won't look so desperate to myself.

8:21pm. Sitting at the counter with the iPad I gave mama for her birthday, I try to remember the last time I saw her use the device. My intention was to give her a way to download books online and maybe even subscribe to a few magazines or newspapers. The online reviews showed this model to be popular for older adults because the backlit screen and adjustable font sizes are easier on the eyes. I had even set it up so that she could try a few audiobooks.

Shame on me for trying to enlighten her with modern technology.

According to her, there is no substitute for the feeling of a real book in your hands, and how do we know the government isn't using the internet to keep track of what we're reading? So, the iPad-as-a-gift was a fail and, rather than let it collect dust on her nightstand, I've been using it for my own entertainment.

While I wait to check my message, I Google '*what does it mean to dream of a snake and a lizard?*'

I had two separate dreams last night, one about an apparently harmless snake, the other about a harmless lizard. I'm saying *apparently harmless* because I touched both of them in the dream, when in real life, I'm deathly afraid of them. Not afraid as in I-prefer-not-to-be-around-them. I mean afraid as in jump-over-a-table, run-through-a-wall, run-my-car-off-the-road afraid.

In both dreams, the reptiles had gotten into the house, first the snake and later the lizard, and I chased them in and out of the rooms, behind dressers and beds, along baseboards, until I caught them. Meanwhile, everyone (not sure who everyone was) lounged around, unfazed by the chase.

I know there is symbolism in dreams. Mama said a dream about fish means someone is pregnant and I've heard all sorts of other explanations for the meanings behind our dreams. I've been obsessed with Googling my dreams lately, hoping I'll have one means I'm getting married and having children soon.

According to Google, if you dream about snakes: *this may represent something that you are afraid of facing, accepting or dealing with in waking life: snakes may symbolize someone or something that you view as threatening to your physical or emotional wellbeing.*

And if you dream about lizards: *this may represent your basic instincts and reactions; it may symbolize one or more fears that you are not dealing with; it may represent someone that you see as cold-blooded or thick-skinned; however, since it sheds its skin, it may also represent rebirth or renewal.*

If you dream about snakes and lizards together: *as two of the oldest and most durable creatures on earth, these may portray the power of your survival instincts, both good and bad.*

Mulling over this information briefly, I bookmark the website and plan to revisit it later. I close the browser and click on Cookie Crush and then jump over to Pinterest, but nothing catches my eye. Next, I open Words with Friends and start a new game.

Three (okay, maybe five) of mama's Lorna Doones disappear before I can come up with a good word using the letter E,L,D,A,R, and O. While Abster 125 ponders his or her next move, I go back to Pinterest and search for new hairstyles, before finally allowing myself to check the time again. 8:32.

So, it was him. And the message simply says, *"whats up?"* That's it. Without any context clues, the message is annoyingly vague. I mean, he hasn't texted me since last Sunday after church, when he normally texts me every day. Today is Thursday.

Having waited another 5 minutes before responding, I text back, *"Nothing. Just cleaning the kitchen."*

And then-- crickets. Nothing else from him. And, after an hour, I want to text him back and ask why he even texted me at all? But I don't. Self-control.

Instead, I get to work, prepping my lunch for tomorrow and shutting the kitchen down for the night, then I grab my phone and the iPad and head for my bathroom. It's my retreat at the end of the day. I light a new, almond-scented candle, begin filling the bathtub, shed my clothes and stand in front of the bathroom mirror.

I'm heavy. At a few ounces over 278 pounds, I've gained about 40 pounds over the last two years. There are stretch marks on my boobs and my butt cheeks. How? Why? I don't have any children. I grab a chunk of my thigh meat and squeeze it. The cellulite disappears. When I release my grip, it returns. I place one hand under each butt cheek and lift, turning sideways to see what it would look like if I were to start doing squats again. I let them drop.

Next, I lean closer to the mirror and study my face from all angles. It's pretty, and I don't mean that in a conceited way. I've always been told that I'm pretty.

No one thinks twice before telling me I'm pretty with a caveat—I have a pretty face for a heavy-set girl.

As I'm using the backside of my hand to push the chubby area under my chin up to my jaw, I pause and listen. For a moment, I wonder if I've heard a noise coming from the hallway, but there is only silence.

I reach over to shut off the bathwater, an action which causes the turkey wing part of my arm and my boobs to swing in unison. I stand again. I lift one arm and try to make a muscle. Then, I wave at myself in the mirror. The turkey wing is jangling and so is the corresponding boob. I slide one hand under each boob, lift, and then push them together. I let them drop. I like my breasts, but they're heavy. Maybe I should check to see if my insurance covers breast lift surgery.

When I lift them up again and turn sideways to see how they'd look if they sat up higher, I definitely hear something from the hallway: "Cent! Cynthia!"

I drop my heavy boobs, grab my robe from the hook behind the door and hurry to her room. I know she doesn't want anything important, but she'll act like somebody's torturing her if I don't come running when she calls.

"What, ma? I was trying to take a bath!"

Her room is dark, but for the bright light of the judge show she's watching on TV. She fumbles around with the remote control, presses a button and the channel changes. Sitting up and reaching for the bedside lamp, she peers at the remote and mumbles to herself.

"Mama! What do you need? I was about to get in the tub."

She presses another button and Judge Mathis reappears on the screen. Another button is pressed, and the volume is silenced. She places the remote on her lap, satisfied, and lies back on her pillows, looking at me.

"Oh. I thought you were in the kitchen and I just want you to bring me some of that Arma Parma."

I'm at a loss as to what she wants. "Some *what*?"

Now, she's frustrated. "Arma. Parma. ArmaParma! Armall Parmall-- I don't know how to say it! I've been in here all day, waiting for you to bring me something to drink and you didn't even come to check on me!"

I can't contain my annoyance. "Mama! Yes I did! I came in here when you were watching Divorce Court and I put those two bottles of water on your nightstand. Now, don't act like you don't remember that! And I don't even know what ArmaParma is!"

She glares at me. I know that I'm hollering, but she just pushes my buttons. It seems like I can just walk into a room-- no, I can hear the sound of her voice-- and I'm instantly irritated. And then I feel guilty. She's my mother. I love her and I would do anything for her. The Bible says to honor and obey your parents. But, Lord, have mercy!

I take a deep breath and relax my shoulders. "What is Arma Parma, mama?"

She dismisses me. "Don't worry about it. I'll drink the water. Go 'head and get your bath."

Guilt won't let me walk away. "No, ma, it's fine. Just tell me what you need."

She picks at her nightgown and mumbles, "I just wanted some of that thing that tastes like lemonade and sweet tea that you had the other day. The one you brought me from Chick-fil-A and you said you could make it at home.

I stand still for a moment, confused, and then I laugh. I bust out laughing and I get so weak that I have to lean on the door frame for support.

"Mama! An Arnold Palmer? It's called an Ar-Nold Palm-Er! What in the world is Arma Parma?" I can barely breathe from the laughing, but I can't stop.

"Come one, Mama! Arma Parma? Now you know that's funny!"

She picks at the edge of her blanket for a second and then picks up the remote control and presses a button, ignoring me.

When I bring the glass of half-sweet tea, half-lemonade back into the room and hand it to her, I hold on for a few extra seconds until she looks at me.

"Here's your Arma Parma, ma'am."

She laughs then, finally, and swats at my backside. "Get on outta here, girl!"

Though I may be a little thicker than I was in my youth, I'm still swift enough to avoid her playful whooping. I scoot just out of her reach and wink at her as I slip out of her room and pull the door closed behind me.

After my bath, I brush and floss, scrub my face, and apply my monthly glycolic facial peel. While I wait for the peel to begin working, I slather shea butter on my feet, pull on my spa socks, and then rub more shea butter over my stretch marks. Next, I slip into panties and an oversized tee shirt, lay across my bed, and tap my phone screen to check for new messages. There are none.

I scroll through Facebook, Instagram, Pinterest, but nothing seems to pique my interest. I return to my text messages and shoot him a one-word message: *wow.*

I watch as tiny bubbles appear under my message and I can tell that he's typing a response, but after a moment, the bubbles disappear, and I'm pissed at myself for waiting for his reply. Then, after I rinse and moisturize my face, just before I power my phone off, he responds:

Him: *Don't be like that.*

Me: *like what?*

Him: *you're mad bc I didn't text you right back.*

Me: *I'm not mad*

Him: *yeah right*

Him: *you can't fault me for stuff like that. That being said, im serious when I say I want to take it slow. I did just get out of a relationship and I don't wanna rush in bc that's not fair to you. But I like being with you and we always have great experiences together.*

Me: *I understand*

Him: *I hope that's okay. I just want to be honest.*

Me: *I know you've been through a lot. I've told you before, I respect your need for more time.*

Him: *I mean I'm not saying I'm closed to us evolving into something more, I just don't want to rush into it!*

Me: *well I'm not going to rush you! I'll let you go at your own pace.*

After I press send, I wait. He doesn't reply but I wait a little longer—so he won't be able to say I'm pressuring him. I lay on my bed, thinking about his fear of getting into a new relationship. I recognize it as fear because, why else, after two years of hanging out with me, does he continue to remind me that he's *just gotten out of a relationship*? How much time does he need?

When I wake up, at 4:15 am, having fallen asleep holding the phone, I see that he hasn't responded. I place it on the charger and go back to sleep.

CHAPTER TWO

When morning comes and I turn on my phone, I'm greeted by a message from the Sprinkle of Jesus app:

Stop accepting things that are unacceptable.

It's the simplest message, but it causes tears to burn behind my eyelids. It's been two years since my friend Ruth died suddenly, but I feel as though I can hear her voice saying the words out loud. *Stop accepting things that are unacceptable.* And she's right. She *was* right.

I can still remember the day she told me to download the app on my phone. She had told me she used daily affirmations to keep her mind focused on the Lord. She'd said I needed to do the same thing: Focus my mind on the Lord and stop worrying about finding a man and having a baby. She'd said those desires would manifest in my life only in God's time and not mine.

I had said, *yeah, but does God realize that I'm almost 40? I'm running out of time to have kids.*

And I remember the way that she had looked when she whispered, *If the Lord saw fit to give Sarah and Abraham a baby at the age of 90, then there ain't nothing he can't do. Genesis 18 and 14 says, Is anything too hard for the Lord?*

I had laughed at first-- I knew the story of how Sarah couldn't conceive and had given up all hope. How she had allowed her husband to make a baby with her servant as a last resort, only to finally conceive a child at the age of 90-- but the laughter had gotten hung up in my throat when I caught a glimpse of Ruth's expression. She was so serious.

That's when I knew that her faith was so much stronger than mine. That's when I knew that I needed to do better. I followed her advice, knowing she'd never steered me in the wrong direction, and downloaded the app.

I'm so thankful for her advice. When the daily messages pop up on my phone, I feel as though she's still here with me. I mean, how could I have known she *wouldn't* be here anymore?

I haven't told anyone about the brokenness I have endured since she left me.

Since she left us.

Since she passed away or the Lord called her home.

Whatever you want to call it-- she's gone. And I am broken.

The loss of a friend, I now understand, is an ailment no one can help you with. *No one but the Lord*, is what she would say about it. *It's me and you, Lord*, she'd probably say, too. And it's true. The death of a dear friend is something people can't understand unless they have experienced it firsthand.

I have learned, the loss of a friend puts you into an unfortunate category which is almost completely unrecognized by society. People will give you their condolences, say they are sorry to hear that such-and-such has passed, ask how it happened, and send prayers up-- but afterwards, they will go on with their lives.

And I'm trying to go on with mine, too. After all, it's not like I lost my mother or my father. It's not like I lost a child or a spouse. But I can't just *go on*. At least, not in the same way. My life has been interrupted. I've been knocked off-course, and I'm getting back on track, so to speak, but I'm not the same as I was before.

Life without Ruth is like this: One time, I broke my pinky toe. Fractured it, actually. And it hurt like the devil, but the doctor couldn't do anything about it. It looked fine on the outside, even though the x-ray showed a hairline fracture.

The doctor said it didn't need a cast, splint, or boot. He said it just needed time to heal, maybe six weeks or so. I was still able to walk on it, and I'm sure I looked alright from the outside, but when I stepped a certain way, when I wore certain shoes, the pain shot through my foot something terrible. Sometimes, it felt like it would never stop hurting, and I contemplated seeing another doctor for a second opinion.

But it did get better, as the doctor had said, even though it still gives me problems every now and then, for instance, when the lady pulls my toes too far apart during a pedicure. Oh! It hurts like a mother, and nobody can see it or understand it except me. So, yeah, I can run again and I can wear heels, but my pinky toe isn't like it was before. It's alright, but it's not okay.

Did you enjoy this sneak peek of Good Morning, Beautiful, the second novel in the Trust series? If so, follow me to find out what happens next!

https://booksbydaines.com/pages/beta-and-book-clubs
https://twitter.com/booksbydaines
https://www.facebook.com/BooksbyDaines/
https://www.instagram.com/booksbydaines/

About the Author

By trade, Daines L. Reed is a registered dental hygienist. By birth, she is a writer, an observer of people, and a lover of words. She cannot live without books and cannot go a single day without asking, "What if?"

Daines writes stories in her head every day, especially during the quiet time she may have while she is working. Through her debut novel, *Trust*, Daines has exposed a cultural issue that needs to be addressed. She hopes this novel will provide the spark for a dialogue that can push individuals to take a more active interest in the legacies they leave for their children.

Made in the USA
Middletown, DE
28 November 2020

25349497R00125